THE STRONGER RELATIONSHIP
COUPLES THERAPY WORKBOOK

YOU DON'T HAVE TO WAIT FOR BOTH OF YOU

A 10-Week Relationship Workbook for the Partner Who's Ready to Begin

Whether you're working through this together or starting alone — this book meets you exactly where you are.

Harper & Lane

How to Use This Book

This is not a book about what's wrong with your relationship. It's a book about what's possible.

Whether you picked this up together, or whether you're the one who always picks things like this up — you are in the right place. This workbook is designed to work for both of you, and for just one of you. It will never require your partner to be on board before you can begin.

Two Tracks, One Journey

Every chapter in this book contains two clearly labeled tracks:
- TOGETHER TRACK — exercises and conversations designed to do as a couple, taking about 20–25 minutes
- SOLO TRACK — reflection prompts and action steps for the partner working through this alone, taking about 20–30 minutes

If your partner joins you later — even halfway through — that's completely fine. The chapters are designed so someone can pick up the book at any point without needing to start from scratch.

The 30-Minute Promise

Every session in this workbook is designed to fit inside 30 minutes. Each chapter is organized around a single weekly theme with:

- One short narrative section to read (5–7 minutes)
- A core exercise or conversation — Together or Solo (15–20 minutes)
- A Weekly Check-In Prompt to close the session (5 minutes)
-

If 30 minutes isn't available this week, a '10-Minute Version' is marked for every chapter — the single highest-impact exercise to do when life is particularly full.

WHAT YOU'LL FIND IN EVERY CHAPTER

LEGEND
WORKBOOK PROMPT — Write-in space for your responses
TIME ESTIMATE — How long this session or exercise takes
SOLO TRACK — Exercises specifically for the partner working alone
CONVERSATION STARTER — Scripts to use in real-time with your partner
CHECKLIST — Quick reference for skills and steps
STORY — A composite couple vignette to illustrate the concept
10-MIN VERSION — The highest-impact exercise when time is short

If someone handed you this book, here's what they're not saying:
You are the problem. I am giving up. I need you to change.

Here's what they are saying:
- *I love us enough to try something new. I am not asking you to do therapy. I am asking for 30 minutes a week to talk about us. That is it.*
- *You don't need to have read anything before this. You don't need to believe workbooks work. You just need to be willing to sit down and try Chapter 1. The rest can wait.*

IMPORTANT: A Word About Safety
This workbook is designed for relationships where both partners feel physically and emotionally safe. If you are experiencing abuse — physical, emotional, or otherwise — please do not use this book with your partner. Instead, reach out to the National Domestic Violence Hotline: 1-800-799-7233 or thehotline.org.

This workbook is a self-help resource, not a substitute for professional therapy. If your relationship involves active crisis, severe trauma, or mental health challenges that significantly impair daily functioning, we encourage you to seek support from a licensed therapist alongside (or before) using this book.

BOOK AT A GLANCE

WEEK	CHAPTER	THEME	KEY SKILLS	WORKBOOK TOOLS
1	01	The Map of Us	Relationship Landscape Map, 5 Dimensions Assessment	Assessment · Scores Debrief · Solo Invitation
2	02	The Story You're Telling Yourself	Attribution Error, Stuck Narratives, CBT Reframing	Narrative ID · What's True? · Solo Reframe
3	03	The Language of Being Heard	Four Horsemen + Antidotes, Soft Startup Formula	Horseman ID · Startup Practice · Unspoken Letter
4	04	The Art of Being Heard	Validation, Emotional Attunement Ladder (EFT)	Attunement Rewrite · Listening Exercise · Rules
5	05	Fighting Differently	Escalation Anatomy, Time-Out Protocol, Repair Attempts	Conflict Map · Time-Out Agreement · Repairs
6	06	Your Partner Is a Stranger	Love Maps, 36 Questions, Bids for Connection	Love Map Update · Bid Tracking · Phone-Free Date
7	07	The Missing Language of Touch	Physical Intimacy Check-In, Desire Discrepancy, 6-Second Kiss	Check-In · Touch Inventory · Physical Origins
8	08	The Weight of Life	Money Origin Stories, Parenting Alignment, Stress Conversation	Money Origins · Parenting Values · Stress Talk
9	09	The Future We're Building	Shared Meaning Pillars, Rituals, Vision Statement	Meaning Map · Vision Statement · 3-Year Vision
10	10	The Relationship You Keep Choosing	ATTUNE Framework, Maintenance Plan, Completion Ritual	Maintenance Plan · Final Session · Completion

The Partner Who Shows Up First

You are not behind. You are not too late. You are not asking for too much. You are the person who decided that love is worth the trouble of being honest about it — and that is where every good thing in a relationship begins.

The Story This Book Was Written For

You didn't fall in love thinking you'd one day be Googling "couples therapy workbook" at 10pm after another conversation that went nowhere.

But here you are. And that matters more than you know.
Maybe it happened gradually — the slow erosion of a Thursday night ritual, the way you stopped finishing each other's sentences, the growing suspicion that you're living alongside your partner rather than with them. Or maybe there was a specific moment: a fight that went too far, a silence that lasted too long, a night when you lay side by side in the dark and felt, for the first time, like strangers.
Either way, you're here. You did what most people don't: you admitted, to yourself at least, that something needs to change. You didn't wait for your partner to suggest it. You didn't wait until the situation became a crisis. You went looking for a way forward.

That is not a small thing.

Most books about relationships assume both partners arrive at the starting line together — equally motivated, equally ready, equally invested in the work. That's a lovely idea. It's also not how it usually goes. Usually, one person gets there first. Usually, one person carries the weight of the relationship's emotional maintenance for longer than feels fair. Usually, one person is reading these words right now while their partner is in the other room, unaware this book even arrived.

This book was written for that person.

For you.

Here is what the research actually says — and it's the kind of thing that, once you hear it, tends to change how you think about the next ten weeks.

Individual change within a relationship almost always precedes relational change.

When one partner shifts — how they listen, how they respond, how they manage their own emotional reactivity — the dynamic between them changes. It has to. A relationship is a system, and when one part of a system begins moving differently, the whole system is required to respond. Not immediately. Not effortlessly. But reliably, over time, when the shift is real and sustained.

This doesn't mean you are responsible for fixing everything. It doesn't mean the problems are yours alone. It means you have more influence over this relationship than you currently believe — even before your partner opens a single page of this book.

This is the quiet power of showing up first.

WHAT THE RESEARCH SHOWS
Couples wait an average of six years after relationship problems begin before seeking any kind of help. Six years. That's six years of accumulated hurt, misunderstanding, distance, and unspoken resentment — before anyone reaches out. You picking up this book right now is, statistically speaking, an unusual act of courage.

Research on Emotionally Focused Therapy (EFT) — one of the most well-validated approaches to couples work in existence — shows that 70 to 75 percent of couples move from distress to recovery through structured therapeutic work. And that one partner's individual growth consistently creates measurable positive change in relationship dynamics, even when the other partner isn't actively engaged.

You are not wasting your time. You are not trying to move something that can't be moved. You are beginning — and beginning is everything.

Meet Maya and Jordan

Throughout this book, you'll follow two people. Their names are Maya and Jordan.

Maya is the one who bought this workbook. She's been carrying a quiet worry about her marriage for about two years — long enough that it no longer feels like worry and has started to feel like furniture. She's not sure when exactly they went from being a couple who stayed up too late talking to a couple who scroll through their phones in separate rooms. But she knows they did.

Jordan didn't buy this book. Jordan doesn't quite see the problem — or rather, Jordan sees it differently. "We're fine," Jordan tends to say. And in many ways they are. The bills get paid. The kid gets loved. There are no dramatic blowups. There's just a kind of gray, low-grade distance that Maya finds unbearable and Jordan has mostly learned to ignore.

Maya and Jordan are not real people. They're a composite — built from patterns that appear again and again in couples therapy offices, in Reddit threads, in the text messages people send their friends at 11pm. Their details have been changed. Their dynamic has not.

You'll meet them at their worst. You'll watch them fumble through the exercises in this book with uneven commitment and occasional resentment. You'll watch something shift. Their story is here not because every couple looks like them — yours may be quite different — but because somewhere in their journey, something will probably look like yours.

📖 MAYA AND JORDAN — THE NIGHT BEFORE SHE FOUND THIS BOOK

The argument had been about the dishwasher, technically. Or it had started as the dishwasher and become something else entirely — something about how Maya always has to notice everything, how Jordan never takes initiative, how this is what every argument turns into, and why do we always end up here?

They'd gone to bed without resolving it. Not angrily — they'd moved past explosive anger years ago — but with that particular silence that means both people have retreated behind their own wall, waiting for the other to make the first move, neither of them making it.

At 11:04pm, Jordan's phone showed Maya was still awake. At 11:07, she was in the bathroom. At 11:09, she was back in bed. Jordan pretended to be asleep.
At 11:32, Maya was on her phone searching "how to communicate better with your partner" and finding, as always, advice that assumed both people wanted to communicate better. She searched for twenty minutes. Then she found this book.

What It Is

This is a structured ten-week program. Each week has a single theme, a 30-minute session, exercises for both individual reflection and joint conversation, and a simple weekly ritual to build connection between sessions. The content is grounded in the most well-researched approaches to couples work available — Emotionally Focused Therapy (EFT) developed by Dr. Susan Johnson, the Gottman Method developed by Drs. John and Julie Gottman, and elements of Cognitive Behavioral Therapy (CBT) adapted for relational work.

This is a book you can use alone. Every chapter has a clearly marked Solo Track — a full set of reflection prompts and action steps designed specifically for the partner who is working through this book without their partner's active participation. If you're using the Solo Track right now, you are not doing a lesser version of this work. In many ways, you're doing the harder version. And you are not alone in it.

This is a book that takes your life seriously. The 30-minute sessions exist because real couples — the ones with jobs and children and aging parents and packed calendars — don't have unlimited time. Every chapter also includes a 10-Minute Version: the single highest-impact exercise to do when a full session isn't possible. Some weeks, 10 minutes is all you've got. That's enough to matter.

What It Isn't

This is not a book that will tell you to stay or to leave. That is not its job. Its job is to help you see your relationship more clearly, communicate more honestly, and approach whatever decisions lie ahead from a place of greater clarity and greater self-respect. What you decide to do with that clarity is entirely yours.

This is not a substitute for professional therapy. For many couples, a structured workbook like this one will be sufficient — and powerful. For others, it will be the thing that reveals the work is deeper than a book can reach, and that a therapist's guidance is the right next step. Both of those outcomes are successes. If you work through this book and conclude that you need more support, that's not a failure. That's wisdom.

This is not a book about what's wrong with you, or with your partner, or with your relationship. Every tool in these pages assumes you and your partner are both trying your best with what you currently know. The goal is to expand what you know — and then to practice something different.

Each chapter is designed to be completed in approximately 30 minutes. Here's how that time breaks down:

5–7 minutes — Read the chapter's narrative section (you can do this before your session if that's easier)
15–20 minutes — Complete the core Together or Solo exercise
5 minutes — Weekly Check-In closing ritual

If you're doing the Solo Track, your sessions may run slightly longer — up to 30 minutes — because solo reflection tends to go deeper. That's expected and good.

You don't have to do a chapter in one sitting. Many couples split the reading and the exercise across two evenings. What matters is completing the full chapter before moving to the next.

Two Tracks, One Direction

Every chapter in this book contains two clearly marked tracks. You choose which one to follow each week — and you can switch between them as your situation changes.

TOGETHER TRACK	SOLO TRACK
Exercises and conversations to do as a couple.	**Reflection prompts and action steps for the partner working alone.**
20–25 minutes	20–30 minutes
Best for:	Best for:
Couples using this book together, or for the chapters where your partner has agreed to join you.	The partner whose other half hasn't joined yet — or isn't sure they will. All ten chapters have a full Solo Track.

If your partner joins you partway through — even in Week 7 or Week 9 — that's completely fine. The chapters are designed so someone can pick up the book at any point without needing to start from the beginning. There is no penalty for a late start. There is only the benefit of beginning.

And if your partner never joins? The Solo Track is not a consolation prize. It is its own complete program. The questions it asks are sometimes harder than the ones in the Together Track. The changes it invites are real, and they are yours — regardless of what your partner chooses to do with them.

The book moves through four phases, each building on the one before.

Weeks 1–2	**FOUNDATION**	Understanding where you are and how you got here. Mapping the relationship honestly. Identifying the stories you tell yourself that keep you stuck.
Weeks 3–5	**COMMUNICATION**	Learning to speak in ways your partner can actually hear. Learning to listen in ways that create safety. Learning to fight without destroying what you're fighting for.
Weeks 6–8	**CONNECTION**	Rebuilding emotional and physical intimacy. Becoming curious about your partner again. Navigating the external pressures — money, parenting, time — that quietly erode connection.
Weeks 9–10	**FORWARD**	Creating shared meaning and a vision of the relationship you're intentionally building. Establishing the habits, rituals, and agreements that make the work last.

You can move at your own pace. Some couples work through two chapters in a week when momentum is high; others spend two weeks on a single chapter when life gets loud or a particular exercise opens a door that takes longer to walk through. Both are fine. There is no wrong pace.

The only pace that doesn't work is standing still.

Most workbooks send you directly to Chapter 1 without asking you anything first. This one wants to do something different. Before you move into the structured ten weeks, take a few minutes — right now, or before your first session — to answer these questions honestly. There are no right answers. There is no one watching. This is just you, deciding what you actually want.

Starting Point — For You, Before Chapter 1

Take your time with these. Write what's true, not what sounds good.

Why did you pick up this book? (Be specific — what happened, or what has been slowly happening, that led you here?)

What are you most afraid of — about this process, about what you might find out, about what might need to change?

What do you actually want for this relationship? Not what you think you should want — what do you actually want?

On a scale of 1–10, how hopeful are you right now that things can genuinely improve? (There's no wrong answer — even a 2 is enough to begin.)

My number: _______

What would make this process feel worthwhile to you, even if it doesn't turn out exactly as you hope?

🌿 SOLO TRACK — STARTING HERE — IF YOU'RE WORKING THROUGH THIS ALONE

There's an extra question for you. Take as long as you need with it.

Your partner doesn't know you're doing this work — or isn't doing it with you yet. That means you're carrying something right now that they aren't: the awareness that things need to change, the discomfort of that awareness, and the weight of being the one who showed up anyway.

Write about that for a moment. Not bitterly — just honestly. What is it like to be the one who showed up first?

And now: What do you hope for yourself from this process — separate from what happens to the relationship? What do you want to understand, or feel, or become, regardless of the outcome?

Keep those answers somewhere. Return to them in Week 10.

A Word About What's Hard

This book will ask things of you that are uncomfortable. Not painful in a harmful way — but uncomfortable in the way that any genuine growth is uncomfortable. It will ask you to look at your own contribution to dynamics you've spent considerable energy blaming on your partner. It will ask you to be curious about someone you may currently feel frustrated with, hurt by, or disconnected from. It will ask you to try things that might not work the first time.

There will be weeks when you open this book and feel resistance — a voice that says this is pointless, nothing will change, you've tried before and it hasn't helped. That voice is not wrong to feel. It has been protecting you. But it has also been keeping you from the thing you most want.

There will probably be a session or two that brings up something bigger than the exercise was designed to hold. If that happens, slow down. It's a signal, not a failure. Appendix C at the back of this book has guidance on when the work has revealed something that needs a therapist's support alongside it.

There will be moments — and this is something experienced couples therapists see consistently — when things get slightly harder before they get better. When you start paying genuine attention to a relationship, things you'd numbed yourself to begin to surface. That's not the workbook making things worse. That's honesty arriving. And honesty, even when it's uncomfortable, is always the beginning of something better.

IF THINGS GET INTENSE DURING A SESSION

It's normal for some exercises to open emotionally charged territory. If a session becomes overwhelming for either partner, use this protocol:
1. Pause the exercise. Say: "I need to slow this down."
2. Take 20–30 minutes apart. Do something genuinely calming — not replaying the conversation.
3. Return to the exercise. The person who called the pause is responsible for coming back.
4. Before resuming, say something that signals you're still on the same team: "I love you even when this is hard."

A Note About Safety

This workbook is designed for relationships where both partners feel physically and emotionally safe. The exercises in this book require a degree of vulnerability — and vulnerability is only possible when the basic condition of safety exists.
If your relationship involves any form of physical violence, coercive control, or abuse — including emotional abuse such as chronic contempt, intimidation, or deliberate humiliation — please do not use this workbook with your partner. These dynamics require specialized professional support, and couples therapy approaches (including this workbook) are not designed for relationships where one person's safety is at risk.
If you are uncertain about whether your relationship qualifies as safe, please reach out for support before proceeding.

☎ IF YOU NEED SUPPORT
National Domestic Violence Hotline: 1-800-799-7233 (call or text) | thehotline.org
Crisis Text Line: Text HOME to 741741
SAMHSA National Helpline: 1-800-662-4357 (mental health and substance use)

If you are outside the US, search for your country's domestic violence hotline.

This workbook is a self-help resource, not a clinical intervention. It is not a substitute for professional therapy. If your relationship involves significant trauma, active addiction, or mental health challenges that substantially impair daily functioning, we strongly encourage working with a licensed therapist alongside (or before) using this book.

One Last Thing Before We Begin

There's a particular kind of loneliness that comes with being the partner who shows up first. The loneliness of caring more, or seeming to. The loneliness of doing this work — or wanting to do this work — while your partner watches television in the next room. The loneliness of not being able to explain to anyone why you're still trying, why you bought another book, why you haven't given up yet.
That loneliness is real. And it doesn't mean you're a fool for staying. It means you haven't confused the difficulty of a relationship with its worth.
The couples who come through hard seasons and build something genuinely good on the other side are rarely the ones who had it easiest. They are, almost without exception, the ones who decided — often one partner first, often the other one slightly reluctantly — that what they had was worth the trouble of being honest about it.

That's what this book is asking of you. Nothing more, and nothing less.

So take a breath. Find your 30 minutes. And let's begin.

"The most important thing in communication is hearing what isn't said."
— Peter Drucker

Chapter 1

The Map of Us

Understanding Your Relationship's Current Landscape

Before you can change where you're going, you need an honest picture of where you are. Not where you hoped to be. Where you actually are.

⏱ 30 minutes total	Session time · can be split across two sittings if needed

🌿 SOLO TRACK — This chapter has its own exercises for the partner working alone. You'll find them in the Solo section below.

What 'Drifting' Actually Means

Most couples don't end up in trouble because of a single catastrophic event. They drift. The drift is quiet, incremental, and almost invisible while it's happening — which is exactly what makes it so disorienting to look up one day and find that you're further from each other than you realized.

The drift happens in the spaces between. In the phone pulled out over dinner instead of a question asked. In the conversation that stays on logistics when it could go deeper. In the tired, distracted half-listening that passes for communication at the end of a long day. None of these moments feel significant on their own. That's the point. The drift isn't made of dramatic moments — it's made of thousands of ordinary ones that accumulate quietly into distance.

John Gottman, one of the world's foremost relationship researchers, calls this the "sliding door" effect: at any given moment, there is a tiny choice available — a bid made, or a bid ignored; a conversation deepened, or let go. Each individual choice is almost meaningless. The accumulated pattern of those choices, over months and years, determines the health of the relationship.

This chapter is not about deciding what went wrong or who is responsible for the drift. That conversation can come later, if it needs to come at all. This chapter is about something more fundamental: seeing clearly where you are right now, as a starting point. You can't navigate somewhere new if you don't know your current coordinates.

So let's find them.

They used to have a thing. Thursday nights, without planning it, had become theirs — pasta from scratch, cheap wine, whatever show they were bingeing. It wasn't a rule. It just kept happening because they both wanted it to.

Then Phoebe arrived. Then the toddler years. Then Jordan's promotion brought late nights at the office three or four days a week. Maya started going to bed at nine to bank sleep before the morning. Thursday became like every other evening: parallel processing of a shared life, barely touching.

Nobody made a decision to stop. The pasta just stopped happening. The wine stayed on the shelf. The show got watched in fragments, alone.

Jordan, when asked about the relationship, said: "We're fine." And they were, technically. Except Maya hadn't laughed — really laughed — with Jordan in more than a year. Except Jordan had started to feel vaguely invisible in his own home, like a useful presence rather than a wanted one. Except both of them had quietly stopped expecting more than management from the relationship.

This is what drift looks like when it's finished settling. Not a crisis. Not a blow-up. Just two people, sharing a life, who have quietly stopped sharing themselves.

Gottman Institute research — built on four decades of studying thousands of couples — identifies five core dimensions that collectively determine the health and trajectory of a committed relationship. These aren't abstract concepts. They're measurable, observable, and — critically — changeable.

Before we do anything else in this workbook, you're going to take an honest reading of where your relationship currently sits across each of these dimensions. Not where you wish it were. Not where it used to be. Where it is right now.

Read through each dimension carefully. Let it land. Don't rush to score it — understanding what each one actually means will make your assessment far more useful.

1

Friendship & Knowledge of Each Other
This is Gottman's concept of the "Love Map" — the mental model each partner holds of the other's inner world. Do you know what your partner is genuinely worried about right now? What they're looking forward to next month? What they most need from you this week but probably won't ask for?

Couples in distress often know each other's logistics perfectly — who's picking up the kids, whose turn it is to call the plumber — and each other's inner worlds very little. When friendship erodes, everything else becomes harder.

2

Emotional Safety & Trust
Can each of you be vulnerable with the other without fear of judgment, dismissal, contempt, or having what you share used against you in a future argument? Emotional safety is not the absence of conflict. It's the presence of the belief that you can speak honestly and be met with care.

When emotional safety is low, partners begin protecting themselves — sharing less, softening difficult truths, or going silent on things that matter. This protection makes sense. It also makes genuine intimacy almost impossible.

Conflict Patterns

All couples have conflict — including healthy ones. The difference between couples who thrive and couples who struggle is not the presence of disagreement but the pattern of it. Does conflict lead to understanding, or does it lead to escalation, withdrawal, and residue that never quite clears?

Gottman's research identified specific conflict behaviors — what he called the Four Horsemen — that predict relationship failure with remarkable accuracy. We'll work directly with these in Chapter 3. For now, simply notice your honest sense of how conflict tends to go in your relationship: does it bring you closer or push you further apart?

Emotional & Physical Intimacy

Intimacy is not simply physical closeness, though physical affection matters deeply. It's the felt sense of being truly known by another person and choosing to stay — and choosing to let them in. Many couples maintain physical routines while losing the emotional intimacy that gives those routines meaning.

When emotional intimacy fades, physical intimacy often follows — not always, but frequently. And when both are low, partners tend to feel like roommates: cooperative but not connected, functional but not close.

Shared Meaning & Future

Do you have a sense of where you're going together? Shared values, shared rituals, a shared vision of the life you're building? Couples who drift often stop constructing a shared future and simply manage a shared present — coordinating logistics rather than cultivating meaning.

Gottman's research found that couples who build a "shared culture" — their own symbols, traditions, ways of understanding the world together — show dramatically higher long-term satisfaction. This dimension asks: are you still building something together, or just maintaining what you have?

WHAT THE RESEARCH SHOWS

Gottman's longitudinal research found that relationship satisfaction is not primarily determined by how couples feel about each other at any given moment — it's determined by the accumulated pattern of small interactions over time. Couples who regularly "turn toward" each other in small, ordinary moments build a reserve of positive sentiment that protects the relationship during difficult periods. Couples who consistently "turn away" deplete that reserve, leaving them vulnerable even when no major crisis is present.
The five dimensions above are not static. Research consistently shows that couples who deliberately attend to these areas — even with modest, consistent effort — can shift their trajectory meaningfully within weeks. That's not optimism. That's what the data shows.

How to Read Your Scores Honestly

Before you fill in the Relationship Landscape Map below, a few things worth naming:

First: there are no right answers. A score of 2 in Emotional Safety is not a judgment — it's information. It tells you where to focus, not what to conclude.

Second: your scores will probably differ from your partner's. This is normal, expected, and actually useful. The gap between how each partner perceives the relationship often tells you as much as the scores themselves. Where you see the same strengths and vulnerabilities, you'll find shared ground to build on. Where you see things differently, you'll find some of the most important conversations this workbook will help you have.

Third: be honest rather than diplomatic. The instinct to score higher than you feel, to protect your partner's feelings or avoid a difficult conversation, is understandable — but it works against you here. This map is only as useful as it is accurate. You're not submitting it to anyone. You're creating a starting point.

Finally: whatever your scores are right now, they represent the present moment. They are not a verdict on the relationship, on your partner, or on whether things can change. They are simply where you are today — and today is where all change begins.

⏱ 20–25 minutes	*Session time · can be split across two sittings if needed*

Complete the Relationship Landscape Map below independently — meaning each of you fills in your own scores without discussing them first. Use the space provided, or each write on a separate sheet if you prefer your responses to stay private until you're ready to share them.

After you've both completed your scores, follow the Conversation Guide below the map.

THE RELATIONSHIP LANDSCAPE MAP

Complete independently. Do not discuss scores until both partners are finished.

PARTNER A	Score
Scale: 1 = very low · 3 = moderate · 5 = very strong	
Friendship & Knowledge	_ _ _
Emotional Safety & Trust	_ _ _
Conflict Patterns	_ _ _
Emotional Intimacy	_ _ _
Shared Meaning & Future	_ _ _

PARTNER B	Score
Scale: 1 = very low · 3 = moderate · 5 = very strong	
Friendship & Knowledge	_ _ _
Emotional Safety & Trust	_ _ _
Conflict Patterns	_ _ _
Emotional Intimacy	_ _ _
Shared Meaning & Future	_ _ _

Looking at your five scores: which dimension feels most urgent to address first, and why?

Is there a score that surprised you — one that felt higher or lower than you expected?

Conversation Guide — Share Your Scores (10–15 minutes)

Once both partners have completed their individual maps, use these questions to guide your conversation. The goal is not to debate each other's scores — it is to understand them.

Share your scores out loud, one dimension at a time. For each dimension:
"Of these five areas, which one feels most important to you right now — and why?"
"Which score surprised you most — in your own ratings, or in mine?"
"Where do we see the relationship similarly? Where do we see it differently?"

Listener's only job during this conversation:
Listen to understand your partner's score — not to correct it, not to defend against it, not to explain yours until they've finished sharing theirs. This conversation is not a debate. It is two people showing each other a map.

One thing I learned about how my partner sees our relationship that I didn't know before:

One area where our perceptions were similar — and what that tells me:

One area where our perceptions differed most — and what I'm curious about in that gap:

Solo Track — For the Partner Working Alone

⏱ 20–25 minutes	*Session time · can be split across two sittings if needed*

Complete the Relationship Landscape Map above on your own — use Partner A for your scores, and in the Partner B column, write what you genuinely believe your partner's scores would be if they completed it right now. This is not about predicting correctly. It's about examining the gap between how you see the relationship and how you imagine your partner sees it.

After completing both columns of the Landscape Map, take your time with these questions:

Which dimension concerns you most right now — and what specifically is happening in that area?

Look at the scores you gave for your partner's perspective. Where do you think you two see the relationship similarly? Where do you think you'd be furthest apart — and what does that gap tell you?

Without self-blame — just honest reflection: what is one thing you have done, or stopped doing, that has contributed to where the relationship is right now?

What is one thing you believe your partner has done, or stopped doing, that has contributed? (Write this without contempt if you can. Try to find the human version of what's underneath their behavior.)

Which dimension do you most want to see change first — and what would that change look like in a typical Tuesday, concretely?

This week, if the opportunity presents itself naturally, consider showing your partner the Relationship Landscape Map. You don't need to make a production of it. You don't need to explain the whole workbook. You can simply say something like:

"Hey — I've been using a workbook to think about us. There's a quick exercise in the first chapter — it takes about five minutes. Would you be willing to do just that part with me sometime this weekend?"

You are not asking them to commit to ten weeks. You are not asking them to read anything or agree with anything. You are asking for five minutes on a Saturday morning.

If they say yes: wonderful. Turn to the Together Track section above and do it together. If they say no or not yet: that's okay. Continue through this workbook on the Solo Track. The work is still real, and it is still yours.

Note what happens here — not to judge the outcome, but to observe it:

📖 Maya and Jordan — The First Session

Maya waited until Sunday morning, when Phoebe was at her parents' and Jordan was on his second coffee. She put the workbook on the kitchen table and said: "I want to show you something."

Jordan looked at the cover. "A workbook?"

"Just one exercise. Five minutes." She'd rehearsed this. "I'm not asking you to read the whole thing. I'm asking you to fill in a grid and tell me what you notice."

Jordan filled in the map. When they compared scores, there was a long silence.

Maya had scored Friendship & Knowledge at 2. Jordan had scored it at 4.

"You think we're fine," Maya said. Not as an accusation — she was too tired for that. More like reading a fact out loud.

Jordan looked at the number she'd given them. "I didn't realize you saw it that way."

"I didn't either, until I wrote it down."

There was more silence. Then Jordan said: "Okay. What does Week 2 look like?"

A word of caution before you close this chapter and carry your scores forward.
Your scores on the Relationship Landscape Map are a snapshot, not a sentence. They show you where the relationship is in this season — not what it is capable of becoming with sustained, genuine attention.

Couples who score low across multiple dimensions have rebuilt strong relationships. Couples who score high have watched those scores erode through inattention. The map is not the territory. It's a tool. Use it as one.
It's also worth naming that the act of completing this assessment together — or completing it alone and becoming more honest with yourself about where things stand — is itself a form of showing up. It requires something of you. That something is exactly what the next nine chapters are going to work with.

You don't need perfect scores to begin. You need honest ones.

You have those now.

Week 1 Closing Ritual

The Weekly Check-In is a brief closing practice at the end of every session. It takes about five minutes. Its job is to mark the end of the workbook time and to create a small moment of appreciation before you return to the rest of your week.

You can do this together or alone. If you're on the Solo Track, the closing ritual is for you — it still counts, and it still matters.

☑ **Week 1 Closing Ritual — 5 Minutes**
☐ Share one thing you appreciated about your partner this week — something small and specific is better than something large and general
☐ Name one thing from this chapter that felt true, or that surprised you
☐ Set your session time for Week 2 — same day, same time if possible (consistency builds the habit)
☐ Optional: write one word that describes how you're feeling about this process right now — not how you think you should feel. How you actually feel.

The word I'd use to describe how I feel about starting this process:

What that word is about:

⚡ 10-Minute Version — When This Is All You Have

If time is short this week, here's the highest-impact version of Chapter 1:

1. Each partner fills in the Relationship Landscape Map independently (3 minutes each).

2. Share one score each — the one that feels most important to name right now.

3. Ask one question: "What does that score tell you?"

4. Schedule the full session for later this week.

Ten minutes well spent will do more than zero minutes deferred indefinitely.

A thought to carry into Week 2:

Awareness is not the same as action. But it is almost always the beginning of it. You now have a clearer picture of where you are. That clarity — however uncomfortable — is the first real thing you've built together in this workbook.

Chapter 2

The Story You're Telling Yourself

Identifying the Narratives That Keep You Stuck

Every relationship problem has two layers: what is actually happening, and the story each person is telling themselves about what is happening. Learning to tell the difference is one of the most important skills in this workbook.

⏱ 30 minutes total	Session time · can be split across two sittings if needed

> ⚡ SOLO TRACK — This chapter has its own exercises for the partner working alone. You'll find them in the Solo section below.

The Lens You're Looking Through

Here is something that changes the way you think about every argument you've ever had with your partner:

The problem is almost never what you think it is.

What you think the problem is — the thing that set off the argument, the behavior that frustrated you, the pattern that drives you to the edge — is almost always the surface. Underneath it is a story. A meaning your mind assigned to what happened, sometimes so quickly that you experienced it as fact rather than interpretation.

Jordan comes home late again. Maya doesn't just observe a fact. She interprets it: He doesn't prioritize us. He's checked out. If he cared about this family, he would have found a way to be here. Jordan, arriving home to Maya's silence, interprets that too: I can't do anything right. No matter what I do, it's never enough. I'm failing her and I don't even know how to stop.

Neither of those interpretations is entirely true. Both of them feel absolutely real to the person holding them. And both of them — not the lateness, not the silence, but the stories attached to them — are what the argument will actually be about.

This is what CBT researchers and couples therapists have found consistently: the stories we tell about our partner's behavior, not the behavior itself, are the primary drivers of relationship distress. The behavior is the trigger. The story is the wound. 31

This chapter is about learning to see the story for what it is — and discovering that you have more power over it than you think.

 Maya and Jordan — The Dinner That Wasn't About Dinner

It started with a text at 6:15pm: "Running behind, probably 8:30 tonight."
Maya read it and felt the familiar drop in her chest. She'd made dinner. Phoebe had already asked twice when Daddy was coming home. It was the third Tuesday in a row.

By the time Jordan walked in at 8:42, Maya had put Phoebe to bed, cleaned the kitchen, and composed a version of herself that was not angry — or not obviously angry — because she was tired of being the one who was always angry. She said "hi" and went to read.

Jordan, reading the "hi" and the disappearing act, felt the familiar tightening: She's doing it again. I work this hard for us and I still can't win. She doesn't see me — she just keeps score.

Neither of them said anything. The evening passed in a cold quiet that both of them had learned to live inside.

Here is what actually happened: Jordan was late. Maya felt hurt. Jordan felt shut out. No one said what they actually needed. Two people, each holding a story about the other that felt like the full truth — and each story making the next evening a little harder than the last.

The Attribution Error — Why We're Hardest on the People We Love

There is a well-documented quirk in human psychology that researchers call the Fundamental Attribution Error. It works like this:

When you do something that falls short — arriving late, snapping irritably, forgetting something important — your mind immediately reaches for context. I was exhausted. I was under enormous pressure. The commute was a disaster. I'm not like this usually. The explanation is situational, external, temporary.

When your partner does the same thing, the explanation your mind reaches for is different. It's dispositional. It points not to circumstances but to character: They don't care. They're irresponsible. This is who they are. The explanation is internal, stable, and damning.

This asymmetry isn't a personality flaw. It's a feature of how human cognition works. We have rich access to our own inner experience — we know exactly why we did what we did — and very limited access to our partner's. So we fill the gap with the most available explanation, which is usually the one that fits the story we've already been telling.

In a relationship that's been under strain for months or years, that story tends to be a negative one. And the more negative the story, the more likely we are to interpret ambiguous behavior through its lens.

This is not about blame. It's about biology — and about awareness. The moment you can catch yourself reaching for a character explanation for your partner's behavior, you have a choice that you didn't have before.

What the Research Shows

Researcher Aaron Beck — one of the founders of Cognitive Behavioral Therapy — found that automatic negative thoughts about a partner are among the strongest predictors of relationship distress, more predictive than the actual behaviors triggering them. He called these thoughts "cognitive distortions": systematic errors in thinking that feel like facts but are actually interpretations.

Gottman's research echoes this from the other direction. He found that what he called "negative sentiment override" — the tendency to interpret even neutral or positive partner behavior through a negative lens when the relationship is distressed — is one of the clearest markers that a couple is in trouble. When someone in negative sentiment override is told their partner is doing something nice, they are likely to attribute it to manipulation rather than genuine care.

The antidote is not forced optimism. It is the deliberate practice of generating alternative explanations — not to excuse behavior, but to expand the range of what seems possible before you react.

The Five Narratives That Create Distance

Over years of working with couples in distress, a small number of recurring narratives keep appearing — stories that feel completely true to the person holding them and that consistently make repair more difficult. See if any of these feel familiar.

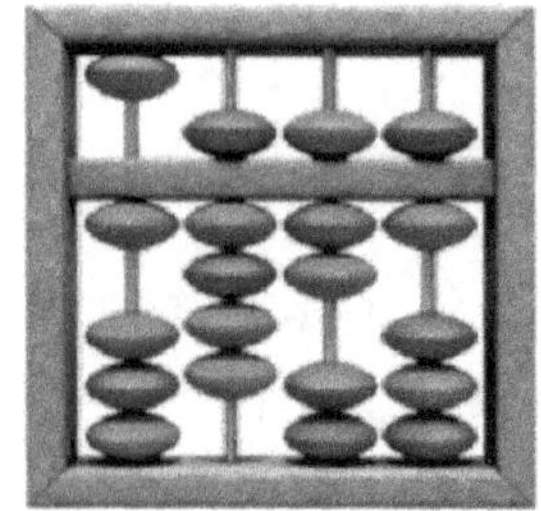

The Scorekeeper

"I do more than they do. I keep track."

The Scorekeeper maintains a running ledger of contributions and slights. Every load of laundry is quietly logged against every forgotten errand. Resentment accumulates invisibly, because the ledger is never shared — it's used as internal evidence that the relationship is fundamentally unfair.

The shift: Relationships are not transactions. When both partners are keeping score, both partners lose. The shift is from "what do I get?" to "what does this relationship need from me right now?"

The Mind Reader

"I already know what they'll say. There's no point."

The Mind Reader has stopped asking and started assuming. They predict their partner's response before the conversation begins — and because they're predicting conflict or dismissal, they often don't start the conversation at all. They confuse their anticipation with certainty.

The shift: Predictions about a partner's response are not facts — they're guesses shaped by past experience and current mood. The shift is from certainty to curiosity: "I think I know, but let me actually ask."

The Catastrophist

"If this doesn't change, we're going to end up like my parents."

The Catastrophist connects every present difficulty to a feared future endpoint. A bad week becomes evidence of a doomed marriage. One unresolved argument is filed as proof that nothing ever gets resolved. The present can't be seen clearly because the future is always catastrophically projected onto it.

The shift: A difficult present is not a determined future. The shift is from projection to presence: "What is actually happening right now — and what would help us in this specific moment?"

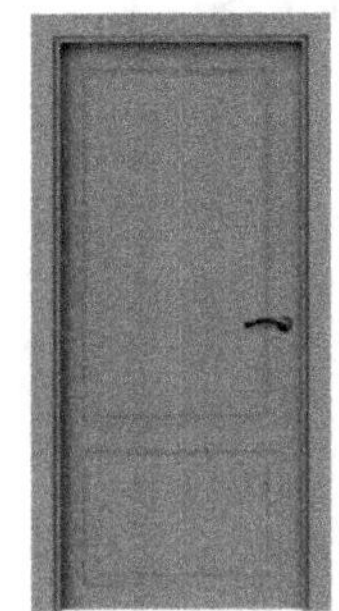

The Avoider
"It's not worth starting a fight over. I'll just let it go."

The Avoider has learned that bringing things up leads to conflict, so they bring fewer and fewer things up. They tell themselves this is the mature, peaceful choice — and in the short term, it is. In the long term, what they're avoiding accumulates. Relationships don't run out of silences. They run out of room for them.

The shift: *Avoidance protects the short-term peace at the cost of the long-term connection. The shift is distinguishing between "letting go" (genuine release) and "burying" (temporary suppression that resurfaces later).*

The Prosecutor
"Everything wrong here traces back to one source: them."

The Prosecutor has assembled a case. Every problem in the relationship has been organized into a coherent narrative in which their partner is the primary cause. They may not consciously think of themselves as a prosecutor — but they have exhibit A, B, and C, and they're ready to deploy them.

The shift: *In a relationship, two people always co-create the dynamic — even when the contributions are unequal. The shift is not from "they're responsible" to "no one is responsible" but to "what is my part, and what can I do with it?"*

A Note Before You Identify Your Narrative

Most people recognize themselves in more than one of these. Most people also recognize their partner in one or two.

The purpose of this exercise is not to label your partner. It is to understand your own most active story — the one that most often runs in the background of your relationship and shapes how you interpret what happens in it.

If you find yourself thinking "yes, but my partner is definitely The Prosecutor" — notice that thought. It might be true. It might also be a version of The Prosecutor thinking.

Check all that apply. Add your own at the bottom if your most active story isn't listed here.

☐ The Scorekeeper ☐ The Mind Reader ☐ The Catastrophist
☐ The Avoider ☐ The Prosecutor

My own version (if different from the above):

Of the narratives you checked, which one is most active — the one that runs most often and most quietly in the background?

Write the specific version of that story — the exact words your mind tends to use. Not a cleaned-up version. The actual running commentary:

How long has this story been running? Can you remember when it started?

The 'What's True?' Exercise — Separating Fact from Story

This is the central exercise of Chapter 2. It's drawn from both CBT and Gottman Method frameworks, and it does one specific thing: it creates a visible gap between what happened and what you told yourself about what happened.

                    That gap is where change lives.

The exercise has three columns. The discipline of the exercise is in Column 1: the Fact. A fact is strictly what a video camera would record — observable, neutral, devoid of interpretation. "She rolled her eyes" is a fact. "She rolled her eyes because she doesn't respect anything I say" is a story. "He left the room" is a fact. "He walked out to punish me" is a story.

Most people find Column 1 the hardest column to fill in, because they've been experiencing their story as fact for so long that separating them feels artificial. It will feel artificial at first. Do it anyway. The practice is the point.

Choose a recent incident — something that happened in the last week or two that left you feeling hurt, frustrated, or disconnected. It doesn't have to be dramatic. Often the most useful incidents are the small ones: a tone of voice, a cancelled plan, a moment of dismissal. Fill in each column as honestly as you can.

▷ The What's True? Exercise

Choose a specific incident from the past week or two. Work through each column before moving to the next.

COLUMN 1 — THE FACT
What actually happened? (Observable only — what a camera would record. No interpretations, no "because," no "as usual.")

COLUMN 2 — MY STORY
What did I immediately tell myself about what it meant? What did I assume about my partner's intentions, feelings, or character?

COLUMN 3 — AN ALTERNATIVE STORY
What is another explanation — equally plausible — that I didn't consider first? (Think about what your most charitable friend would suggest. Think about what context from your partner's week might explain the behavior.)

THE REFLECTION
If you had led with the alternative story instead of your first one, how might you have responded differently? What would that have made available.

Column 1 The Fact	Column 2 My Story	Column 3 An Alternative Story
What actually happened — strictly observable, no interpretation at all	*What I immediately told myself about what it meant*	*Another explanation, equally plausible, that I didn't consider first*

The Reflection

The What's True? table is a tool you can return to throughout the workbook — and beyond it. Any time you find yourself in a loop of the same frustrated thought about your partner, this is the exercise to reach for.

You don't always need to write it out. After practice, you can run the three columns mentally in real time: "That's the fact. That's my story. What else could be true?" Some couples find a shorthand that works in the middle of tension — one partner saying quietly, "Column Three?" as a reminder to both of them.

The Story Beneath the Story

There's something worth naming about why these narratives are so persistent, and why simply "thinking differently" doesn't always make them go away.

Most of the stories we tell in relationships aren't original. They were written earlier — in the families we grew up in, in the relationships we watched or experienced before this one, in the earliest lessons we received about what love looks and feels like when it's real and when it's threatened.

Maya's story — He doesn't prioritize us — is not just about Jordan coming home late. It's connected to something older: a childhood in which people who said they'd be there often weren't, and in which absence felt like a verdict on her worth. Jordan's story — I can't do anything right — is connected to something older too: a family system in which love felt conditional on performance, in which being good enough was a moving target.

Neither of them consciously knows this when they're standing in the kitchen at 8:42pm. They just feel what they feel. But those feelings are operating on a frequency set long before they ever met.

We will come back to origins — yours and your partner's — more directly in Chapter 8 when we explore the external pressures and personal histories that shape relationship dynamics. For now, what's useful to know is this: when a small thing hits you with disproportionate force, the disproportionality is usually information. It's telling you the small thing is touching something larger.

That doesn't mean your feelings aren't valid. It means they're worth being curious about, rather than just acted upon.

Maya did the What's True? exercise on the Tuesday night dinner. In Column 1, she wrote: "Jordan texted at 6:15 saying he'd be back at 8:30. He arrived at 8:42."

In Column 2, she wrote: "He doesn't think we matter. He knows I've made dinner and he still doesn't make it home. He's checked out. I've been trying for months and he's barely even noticing."

She sat with Column 3 for a long time.

Finally she wrote: "He's been working these hours for six months and he hasn't taken a single sick day. He comes home looking exhausted. It's possible — I don't actually know this, but it's possible — that he's working this hard because he thinks that's how he shows he cares. It's possible he doesn't know I need something different."

The Column 3 version didn't make Tuesday night hurt less. But it did something else: it made Jordan a person again, instead of a symbol of everything wrong with the relationship.

The next morning, she said: "I don't think you know what I actually need from you. Can I tell you?"

Jordan looked up from his coffee. "Yeah," he said. "I'd really like to know."

Together Track — Session 2

⏱ 20 minutes total	*Session time · can be split across two sittings if needed*

This session has a single, simple structure. It asks more courage than it appears to require.

Each partner shares one story they have been telling themselves about the relationship — not a complaint, not an accusation, but an honest account of a narrative they recognize running in the background. Use the sentence frame below. Then switch.

The listener has one job: do not defend yourself. This is not the moment to correct the story or explain your side. You will have space for that in Chapter 3. Right now, your only task is to stay present and let your partner's experience land — even if it lands uncomfortably.

💬 Sentence Frame — The Story I'm Telling Myself

Each partner takes a turn completing this sentence:

"The story I've been telling myself is

The part that might not be completely true is

Take your time. The first draft of this sentence often isn't the real one. Sit with it for a moment before you speak.

➡ After the Exchange — What We Noticed

What was it like to share your story out loud?

What was it like to hear your partner's story — without defending yourself?

Was there anything in your partner's story that surprised you, or that you hadn't considered before?

The solo work in Chapter 2 goes to a slightly deeper place than the Together Track. You have the advantage of privacy — use it to be more honest than you might be able to be with a partner present.

🌿 SOLO TRACK — The Story You Want to Let Go Of

Complete the What's True? exercise above using a recent incident. Then take your time with these questions.

What is the most persistent negative story you tell yourself about your partner — the one that surfaces most often and feels most "true"?

How long have you been telling this story? Try to trace it back — did it begin with something that happened early in the relationship? Something from before?

What does holding this story protect you from? (Every persistent story is protecting something — from disappointment, from vulnerability, from having to ask for something you're afraid won't come.)

What would it cost you to let go of this story — even partially, even experimentally?

What would become possible in the relationship if you held the story more lightly?

This week, when you notice your most active narrative running — the Scorekeeper adding things up, the Mind Reader predicting the outcome, the Catastrophist jumping to the worst case — try this:

Pause. Name it silently: "There's the story."

Then ask Column Three: "What else could be true?"

You don't have to believe Column Three. You don't have to act on it immediately. You just have to hold it alongside the story you're already telling — and notice what that does to the next moment. At the end of the week, note what you observed:

What This Week Is Really About

Naming your story doesn't make it disappear. In fact, if you try to force it away, it will almost certainly come back louder.
What changes is your relationship to the story. Instead of living inside it, you start to be able to step outside it occasionally — just long enough to see that it is a story, not a fact. And in that small space between the stimulus and your response, something becomes possible that wasn't there before.

Viktor Frankl called that space the last human freedom: the ability to choose your response. In the context of a relationship, it's more modest than that. It's just the ability to pause long enough to ask: "Is this what's actually happening — or is this what I'm afraid is happening?"
That question won't always change what you do next. But it will sometimes. And sometimes is where everything begins.

Week 2 Closing Ritual

☑ Week 2 Closing Ritual — 5 Minutes
☐ Share one moment this week when you noticed a story running — and what you chose to do with it
☐ Name one thing you gave your partner the benefit of the doubt on this week, however small
☐ Set your session time for Week 3 — pencil it into your calendar now
☐ Optional: name one narrative you'd most like to hold more lightly going forward

Optional — The Narrative I'm Working With
The story I most want to hold more lightly going into Week 3:

If time is short, here's the most important thing you can do from Chapter 2 this week:

Choose one recent moment of friction — something small. Run it through the three columns mentally or on paper:

The Fact (what actually happened, stripped of interpretation).

My Story (what I immediately told myself it meant).

An Alternative Story (what else could be true).

That's it. Even doing this once this week will shift something. The practice builds.

A thought to carry into Week 3:

The story you've been telling yourself about your relationship is not wrong to have. It made sense given what you've experienced. What changes now is that you've seen it — and seeing it means you can begin to work with it, rather than simply living inside it.

Chapter 3

The Language of Being Heard

How to Speak So Your Partner Can Actually Listen

The biggest communication problem in most relationships isn't that people don't say enough. It's that they say the right things in ways that guarantee they won't be heard.

| ⏱ 30 minutes total | *Session time · can be split across two sittings if needed* |

> ✎ SOLO TRACK — This chapter has its own exercises for the partner working alone. You'll find them in the Solo section below.

Why Good Communication Fails

You already know the theory. You've heard it before: use "I statements." Listen actively. Don't interrupt. Reflect back what you hear.

You know this — and yet the same conversation spirals into the same argument. The same look crosses your partner's face. The same wall goes up. The same things get said that nobody actually wants to say, and the same things don't get said that matter most.

Here is what communication training almost always gets wrong: it teaches technique without addressing intention. It gives you the tools without asking what you're trying to build.

In most difficult relationship conversations, the goal — underneath the stated content — is not actually to be understood. It's to be right. To not be blamed. To get your partner to see things your way, or at least to stop seeing things in a way that feels threatening. The goal is to win, or at minimum, to not lose.

And here is the problem: the communication techniques you already know don't work in service of winning. They only work in service of connecting. Use active listening as a tactic to prove your partner wrong, and your partner will feel it. Use the "I statement" formula while still trying to assign blame, and the formula will fail — because the intention defeats the tool.

This chapter doesn't give you more techniques. It gives you something harder and more useful: a different understanding of what you're actually trying to do when you open your mouth in a difficult moment with your partner.

📖 MAYA AND JORDAN — THE SAME FIGHT, TWO DIFFERENT OPENINGS

Maya had been rehearsing the conversation for three days. When Jordan sat down on the couch Thursday evening, she was ready.

Version 1 — the opening she'd been building for three days: "You never prioritize this family. I'm alone in this marriage and you don't even notice. I've been saying this for two years and nothing changes."

Jordan felt the familiar tightening in his chest. The familiar sense of arriving already convicted. He didn't say anything — which Maya interpreted as more proof of the very thing she'd just said.

The conversation lasted forty minutes and resolved nothing.

Three weeks later, after Chapter 2, Maya tried again. Same issue. Different opening: "I've been feeling really lonely lately, and I don't think I've told you that clearly. When you're not home for dinner most nights, I feel like I'm doing this by myself — and what I'd love is to feel like we're a team again. I don't know if that's possible right now, but I wanted you to actually know that's what I need."

Jordan sat forward. "I didn't know it felt like that to you," he said. "I thought you were angry at me. I didn't know you were lonely."

Same problem. Same need. Completely different conversation.

The Four Horsemen — and What to Do Instead

Gottman's research team spent decades studying couples in conflict — watching, recording, coding thousands of conversations to find the patterns that distinguished couples who stayed together from those who didn't. What they found was a set of four specific communication behaviors that predict relationship failure with remarkable accuracy. He named them, somewhat dramatically but memorably, the Four Horsemen.

Each Horseman has an antidote — a direct counter-move that doesn't require your partner to change first. These antidotes are things you can practice starting this week, on your own, regardless of how your partner is communicating.

CRITICISM

Attacking your partner's character rather than describing a specific behavior. The tell is language that makes the problem about who they are — not what they did.

✗ *"You're so irresponsible. You never think about anyone but yourself."*
✓ *"I was really frustrated when the bill didn't get paid. Can we figure out a system so that doesn't happen again?"*

Antidote — The Gentle Start-Up: Describe a specific behavior ("when you..."), name your feeling, and make a positive request. Attack the situation, not the person.

CONTEMPT

Communicating superiority, disgust, or mockery — eye-rolling, sneering, sarcasm that demeans, dismissing your partner's perspective as beneath consideration. Gottman considers this the single most toxic Horseman. It signals that you've stopped seeing your partner as an equal.

✗ *"Oh, that's a great idea. Really brilliant. I don't know why I even bother talking to you."*
✓ *"I hear what you're suggesting. I see it differently — can I share my thinking?"*

Antidote — The Culture of Appreciation: Build a daily habit of noticing and naming what you genuinely appreciate about your partner. Contempt grows in a deficit of goodwill. Appreciation is the preventive medicine.

DEFENSIVENESS

Counter-attacking or playing the victim in response to feedback or complaints — instead of taking any responsibility for your part, however small. Defensiveness communicates: "The problem isn't me. It's you." It stops a conversation the other person needed to have.

✗ *"I only forgot because you never remind me about anything. You expect me to be a mind-reader."*
✓ *"You're right — I dropped the ball on that. What would help for next time?"*

Antidote — Taking Responsibility: Find the grain of truth in what your partner is saying and own it explicitly, even if you only agree with part of it. Partial responsibility accepted is better than total responsibility denied.

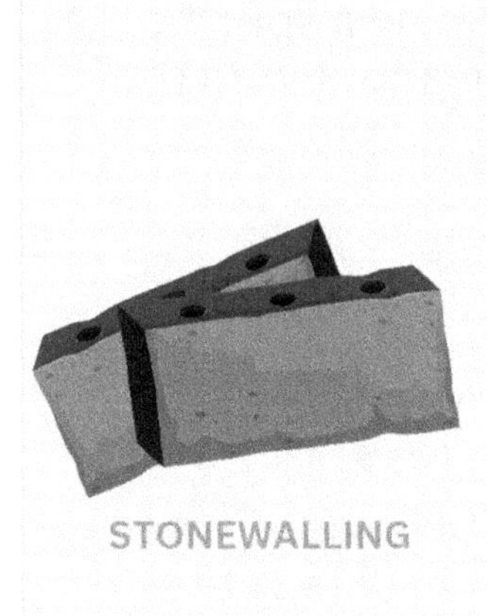

Shutting down, withdrawing, becoming a stone wall — the conversation continues but one partner has physiologically checked out. Usually appears as silence, monosyllables, or sudden "busyness." Stonewalling most often happens when someone is flooded — their nervous system is overwhelmed — and it's less a choice than a physiological shutdown.

✗ *"[Complete silence. Looking at phone. Clipped one-word answers.]"*
✓ *"I'm getting overwhelmed. Can we take twenty minutes and come back to this?"*

Antidote — Physiological Self-Soothing: When flooded, stop. Take a genuine 20-minute break — not to rehearse arguments but to actually calm your nervous system. Then return to the conversation.

WHAT THE RESEARCH SHOWS

Gottman found that Contempt is the single strongest predictor of relationship dissolution — more predictive than any other factor he studied. Couples who expressed contempt for each other in conflict were measurably more likely to separate, and were also more likely to report health problems over time. Contempt is corrosive in every direction.

He also found that Stonewalling — which looks passive — is typically a symptom of physiological flooding: heart rate above 100 beats per minute, cortisol flooding the system, rational thinking significantly impaired. You cannot problem-solve while flooded. The antidote is not willpower. It is a genuine pause.

The good news: each of these patterns is learnable in the opposite direction. Criticism can become a Soft Startup. Contempt can become appreciation. Defensiveness can become ownership. Stonewalling can become a structured time-out. Not perfectly, not immediately — but consistently, with practice.

Which Horseman Is Most Active for You?

Be honest with yourself here. Not which one your partner uses — which one you reach for.

The Horseman I use most when things escalate:
☐ Criticism   ☐ Contempt   ☐ Defensiveness   ☐ Stonewalling

The Horseman I think my partner uses most:
☐ Criticism   ☐ Contempt   ☐ Defensiveness   ☐ Stonewalling

Write a recent example of when you used your Horseman — the actual words or actions, as honestly as you can remember them:

Now write what the antidote version would have looked like in that same moment:

What made the antidote version harder to reach for in that moment?

The Soft Startup — The Most Important Sentence You'll Learn

Gottman's research found something that sounds almost too simple to be true: the way a conversation begins predicts, with more than 96 percent accuracy, how it will end. Not sort of predicts — nearly perfectly predicts.

A harsh startup — an opening that comes in with criticism, blame, or contempt — will almost always end in an unresolved argument, regardless of how the conversation was handled afterward. A soft startup — one that begins with your feeling, a specific situation, and a positive request — creates the conditions under which your partner can actually hear you.

This doesn't mean the Soft Startup is a magic formula that will make your partner receptive every time. It means you've done your part. You've given the conversation the best possible chance. What your partner does with that is theirs to work on.

Here is the formula. It looks simple. It is not easy.

STEP 1 Name a feeling	Start with "I feel..." — a genuine emotion, not a thought or a judgment. "I feel overwhelmed" works. "I feel like you don't care" is a thought dressed as a feeling.
STEP 2 Describe the specific situation	"...when [specific observable behavior or situation]." Be concrete. "When you didn't text me yesterday" works. "When you're always dismissive" doesn't — it's a pattern accusation, not a situation.
STEP 3 State what you need	"...and what I'd love is [specific, positive request]." Ask for what you want, not for what you want them to stop doing. "I'd love to feel like a priority sometimes" is cleaner than "I need you to stop ignoring me."
STEP 4 What to leave out	No "you always" or "you never." No character judgments ("you're selfish"). No bringing up past incidents. No sighs, eye-rolls, or tones that contradict the words. This is a beginning, not a verdict.

THE SOFT STARTUP IS NOT WEAKNESS

Some people resist the Soft Startup because it feels like letting the other person off the hook — like being too gentle about something that genuinely hurt. This is worth naming directly.

The Soft Startup is not softer on the issue. It's softer on the person. You are still raising the thing that matters. You are still asking for something to change. What changes is that you're delivering the message in a form your partner's nervous system can actually receive — rather than one that activates their defenses before you've finished your first sentence.

Hard startups feel satisfying in the moment and almost always make things worse. Soft startups feel vulnerable in the moment and almost always make things better. This is the trade.

Hard Startup vs. Soft Startup — Side by Side

The same need, expressed two different ways. Notice how the left column puts your partner on trial. The right column opens a door.

✕ HARD STARTUP	✓ SOFT STARTUP
"You never help around the house. I do everything."	*"I feel overwhelmed lately, and when the house stuff falls entirely on me, I feel invisible. What I'd love is to figure out a split that works for both of us."*
"You're always on your phone when I try to talk to you."	*"I feel disconnected from you lately. When I'm talking and you're on your phone, I feel like what I'm saying doesn't matter. I'd love to have your full attention for our evening catch-up."*
"You clearly don't care about this relationship as much as I do."	*"I've been feeling lonely inside this relationship, and I don't think I've said that clearly. What I'd love is for us to find some way to feel more like partners again."*
"Why do you always shut down whenever I try to talk about something important?"	*"When our conversations stop before we've resolved anything, I feel frustrated and stuck. I'd love to find a way to keep talking even when it gets hard. Can we try that?"*

Practice — Rewrite a Real Complaint as a Soft Startup

Choose something you've been wanting to raise with your partner — something you haven't known how to say, or have said in a way that didn't land.

The complaint as you've been saying it (or thinking it):

Now rewrite it using the Soft Startup formula:
I feel

____

____

when

____

____

and what I'd love is

____

____

What was harder about writing the Soft Startup version? What did you have to let go of to get there?

Is there a moment this week you could use this? (Not the whole conversation — just this one opening.)

Why This Feels Harder Than It Looks

If you've been trying to write a Soft Startup and finding that it feels stiff, or dishonest, or like you're being asked to apologize for having feelings — you're experiencing something very common.

The Soft Startup requires you to locate and name a genuine feeling, which assumes you have access to your feelings in the moment. Many people don't — not because they don't have feelings, but because years of managing conflict by staying controlled, staying rational, or staying angry have created a significant distance between them and their inner emotional experience.

It requires you to make a specific, positive request — which assumes you know what you actually need, and believe you're allowed to ask for it. Many people have never been explicitly taught that their needs in a relationship are legitimate and worth stating.

And it requires you to remove character judgment from your opening — which means giving up the part of the complaint that feels most satisfying to say, even though it's the part that reliably makes everything worse.

These aren't technique failures. They're places where the workbook is revealing something real about the way you learned to be in relationship. Notice them. Be curious about them. We'll come back to origins in Chapter 8. For now, the practice is simply to try — imperfectly, awkwardly, one conversation at a time.

Maya sat down to do the practice exercise. She stared at "I feel..." for a long time. She'd been telling herself the story — The Scorekeeper, she recognized from Chapter 2 — that Jordan didn't care. Writing "I feel lonely" felt like giving something up. Like admitting she needed him in a way that felt uncomfortably vulnerable.

She almost wrote "I feel like you're checked out" — but she'd learned enough by now to know that was a thought, not a feeling.
She wrote "lonely" and sat with the word for a moment. It felt uncomfortably accurate.

Then: "when you're not home for dinner." Specific. Factual. No accusation.

Then: "and what I'd love is to feel like we're still building something together."

She read it back. It didn't feel like her — not the version of herself she'd been inhabiting for the last two years. It felt younger, softer, more open to being hurt.

She thought: maybe that's the version that can actually be reached.

Together Track — Session 3

⏱ 20 minutes total	Session time · can be split across two sittings if needed

This session has two movements. In the first, each partner takes a turn sharing a Soft Startup version of something they've been wanting to say but haven't known how to — or haven't been able to say in a way that was heard. In the second, the listener responds using the framework below. Read the Listener's Response Framework before you begin. The listener's job in this session is one of the hardest things in this book.

💬 THE LISTENER'S RESPONSE FRAMEWORK

When your partner shares their Soft Startup, your response has three parts — in this order, always:

Step 1 — Reflect: "What I'm hearing you say is..." Repeat back the essence of what your partner shared — in your own words, not theirs. This is not parroting. It's showing that you were actually listening.

Step 2 — Validate: "That makes sense because..." Find the logic of your partner's experience and name it. You do not have to agree with their interpretation. You do have to acknowledge that their feeling makes sense given their experience.

Step 3 — Respond: "Here's what I want you to know..." Now you may share your own reaction, perspective, or response — but only after you've done Steps 1 and 2.

Critical note: Reflecting and validating does not mean you agree. It means you have understood. Understanding must happen before responding — every time. If you respond before reflecting and validating, you have not yet responded to what your partner actually said.

One partner shares their Soft Startup (2–3 minutes). The listener responds using the framework above. Then switch. The full session should take about 20 minutes. If a Soft Startup opens into a bigger conversation that both partners want to have, let it.

That's the point.

What was it like to share your Soft Startup out loud?

What was it like to listen using the framework — without defending or explaining yourself until Step 3?

Was there anything your partner said that landed differently than you expected?

Solo Track — For the Partner Working Alone

The solo work in Chapter 2 goes to a slightly deeper place than the Together Track. You have the advantage of privacy — use it to be more honest than you might be able to be with a partner present.

🌿 SOLO TRACK — WRITE THE CONVERSATION YOU HAVEN'T HAD
There is something you have been wanting to say to your partner — something important, something that keeps coming up inside you, something you haven't found the right way to say. Write it here.

First: write it the way it usually sounds in your head (the version you haven't said because you know it won't land well):

Now: rewrite it as a Soft Startup.

I feel ____ when

____ and what I'd love is

____.

Read both versions back. What's different about how each one feels — to write, and imagining how your partner would receive it?

Is there a moment this week where you could share the Soft Startup version? You don't need to explain the workbook or show them this page. You can simply say the sentence.

Even without your partner here, you can practice the Listener's Response Framework using a recent moment when they were upset and you didn't respond the way you wished you had.

What did your partner say or express? (As objectively as you can remember it.)

What did you actually say or do in response?

Now write the three-step response you wish you'd given:
Step 1 — Reflect: "What I'm hearing you say is..."

Step 2 — Validate: "That makes sense because..."

Step 3 — Respond: "What I want you to know is..."

What gets in the way of responding this way in real time? What would you need to feel, believe, or let go of to be able to do this more consistently?

What This Week Is Really About

Chapter 3 asks something that Chapter 2 prepared you for: to change not just what you say, but why you're saying it.

The Soft Startup only works if you're genuinely trying to connect — not to win, not to be validated in your grievance, not to make your partner feel the weight of what you've been carrying. It works when the goal is for your partner to actually know what's going on for you, and to have the chance to respond to that honestly.

This is a subtle but enormous shift. It means giving up the satisfaction of the hard startup — the accusation that lands, the grievance that finally gets named in all its force — in exchange for something less cathartic and more effective.

Most people find the Soft Startup awkward for the first several attempts. The words feel stiff. The vulnerability feels exposed. That's not a sign you're doing it wrong. That's a sign you're doing something new.

The Listener's Response Framework is equally new for most people. You've spent years learning to protect yourself in difficult conversations — to defend, to explain, to counter. Being asked to simply reflect and validate before responding is asking you to suspend that protection. It's asking you to trust that your side of the story will still get to exist, even if you hold it for a moment while your partner's lands.

It will. Your side still gets to be told. Just not first.

Week 3 Closing Ritual

☑ **WEEK 3 CLOSING RITUAL — 5 MINUTES**
☐ Share one moment this week where you tried something from this chapter — a Soft Startup, a different opening, the Listener's framework
☐ Name one moment where you caught one of the Four Horsemen in yourself — and what you did with that awareness
☐ Appreciation: tell your partner one specific thing you noticed about them this week
☐ Set your session time for Week 4 — same day, same time if possible

Optional — One Thing I Want to Keep Practicing
From Chapter 3, the skill I most want to keep working on this week:

One situation coming up this week where I could try it:

⚡ **10-MINUTE VERSION — WHEN THIS IS ALL YOU HAVE**
Two things, in ten minutes:
1. Identify your primary Horseman. Write one recent example of using it.
2. Write one Soft Startup for something currently unresolved between you and your partner.
You don't have to deliver the Soft Startup this week. You just have to write it.
Writing it is the first change.

Changing how you speak does not mean swallowing what you feel. It means finding the form that gives what you feel the best possible chance of being received. Your feelings deserve that chance. So does your partner — the chance to actually hear you, instead of defending against you.

Chapter 4

The Art of Being Heard

Active Listening, Emotional Attunement, and the Power of Validation

Most people listen to respond. This chapter is about learning to listen to understand — which turns out to be a completely different skill, and a far rarer one.

| ⏱ 30 minutes total | Session time · can be split across two sittings if needed |

> 🌱 SOLO TRACK — This chapter has its own exercises for the partner working alone. You'll find them in the Solo section below.

The Paradox at the Heart of Communication

Chapter 3 was about how you speak. This chapter is about something harder.

Here is one of the most consistently reported findings in couples therapy research: in the majority of relationship conflicts, both partners feel unheard. Simultaneously. In the same conversation.

Both people leave feeling like the other one wasn't listening. Both people feel like they did most of the listening. Both people feel unseen.

This paradox contains an important truth: feeling heard and being heard are not the same thing. And the gap between them is almost never about one partner not trying hard enough to communicate. It's about both partners trying very hard to communicate — and neither of them actually listening.

Listening — real listening, the kind that makes someone feel genuinely received — is not the same as being quiet while the other person talks. It is not waiting for your turn. It is not nodding while internally composing your response. It is an active, effortful, disciplined practice that almost no one does naturally and almost everyone believes they already do.

This chapter is about the gap between what we think listening is and what it actually requires. And it's about why getting this right changes more in a relationship than almost anything else you can do.

They'd had a conversation — if you could call it that — about Maya's mother coming to visit. Jordan had listened, in the sense that he'd been in the room while Maya was talking. He'd offered solutions. He'd pointed out that her mother's visits always went better than Maya expected. He'd suggested she was catastrophizing.

Maya felt more alone after the conversation than before it.

Later, Jordan told a friend: "I don't know what she wants from me. I tried to help and she just shut down. I can't win."

Maya told her sister: "He doesn't actually hear me. He just tries to fix everything. I don't need it fixed. I just need him to understand."

Both of them were right. Jordan was listening. Maya didn't feel heard. These are not contradictions — they are the description of a couple in which one person is speaking and the other is processing, rather than receiving.

The skill this chapter teaches is the difference between those two things.

What Validation Actually Is — and What It Isn't

Validation is the single most powerful communication tool in intimate relationships. It is also the most consistently misunderstood.

When most people hear the word "validation," they hear "agreement." They think: if I validate my partner's feeling, I'm saying they're right. I'm saying their interpretation is accurate. I'm letting them off the hook, or putting myself on it. None of that is what validation means.

Validation means: "I understand that your experience is real and makes sense given your perspective." That's it. It is an act of recognition, not agreement. You can validate your partner's feelings while completely disagreeing with their conclusions. You can say "I understand why you felt dismissed in that moment" without accepting that you were dismissive. You can say "that makes sense that you'd feel hurt by that" without conceding that the hurt was deserved or that your behavior was wrong.

The distinction is not semantic. It changes everything about how conversations unfold.

When someone feels validated, their nervous system settles. The urgency to be heard — which is driving most of the intensity in a difficult conversation — begins to ease. And when that urgency eases, the conversation becomes capable of going somewhere new.

When someone feels invalidated — when their feelings are dismissed, corrected, minimized, or argued with — the urgency intensifies. They repeat themselves. They push harder. They escalate, not because they're unreasonable, but because they haven't yet been received.

Validation is not a technique for getting your partner to calm down. It is the honest acknowledgment that another person's interior experience is real. When you offer it genuinely, it works — not because it's a tool, but because it's true.

WHAT THE RESEARCH SHOWS

EFT researcher Sue Johnson found that emotional responsiveness — the degree to which a partner feels their emotional signals are received and responded to — is the single strongest predictor of relationship security and satisfaction over time. More than communication style. More than conflict frequency. More than shared values. When people feel emotionally responded to, they feel safe. When they don't, they feel alone — regardless of how much they are technically communicated with.

Gottman's research reached a similar conclusion from a different angle: in his analysis of what distinguished the "Masters" of relationships (couples in lasting, satisfying partnerships) from the "Disasters," the key variable was what he called "emotional attunement" — the ability to notice, turn toward, and genuinely respond to a partner's emotional bids and states.

What both bodies of research point toward is the same thing: being heard is not primarily an intellectual experience. It is a felt, bodily, emotional one. You know when you've been heard. And you know when you haven't — even if the other person was technically listening.

The Emotional Attunement Ladder

EFT describes emotional attunement as a five-rung ladder. Each rung builds on the one before it. Most couples in distress get stuck between rungs one and two — they notice something is happening, and they immediately skip to problem-solving, defending, or responding — without completing the middle rungs that actually make the response land.

Read through the ladder carefully before you use it. The sequence matters. These are not interchangeable steps.

1	**Notice** *"I can see that you're upset."*	The first and most basic act: registering that something is happening for your partner emotionally, before you do anything else. This sounds elementary. In practice, many people skip straight to solving, defending, or responding — without first pausing to actually see that their partner is struggling.
2	**Reflect** *"What I'm hearing you say is..."*	Repeat back the essence of what your partner shared — in your own words, not theirs. This is not parroting. It's demonstrating that you were actually receiving what was said, not just waiting for your turn. Most couples get stuck here: they hear the words but interpret them immediately through their own lens, which is why the reflection so often sounds wrong to the person who said it.
3	**Validate** *"That makes sense because..."*	Find the internal logic of your partner's experience and name it out loud. Not "that makes sense because you're right" — but "that makes sense given your history, your fears, what you've been carrying." Validation is the act of making someone's feelings feel legitimate without requiring yourself to agree with their conclusions.
4	**Empathize** *"I imagine that felt..."*	Step into your partner's experience and name the feeling, not just the thought. This is the rung most people find hardest: it requires you to imagine being inside your partner's skin, particularly when you don't agree with their interpretation of events. The word "imagine" is deliberate — you're not claiming certainty about their inner state. You're making a genuine attempt to feel toward them.
5	**Respond** *"And here's where I am..."*	Only now — after you have noticed, reflected, validated, and empathized — do you share your own reaction, perspective, or response. This is not suppression of your own experience. It is sequencing. Your experience is still real and still gets to be named. It simply cannot come before your partner has felt heard.

Rung 3, Validate, is the most consistently skipped step in difficult conversations — and its absence is usually what makes the other person feel unheard even when their partner is genuinely trying.

Skipping validation typically sounds like: jumping straight from "I hear you say you're frustrated" (Rung 2) to "but what actually happened was..." (a response that bypasses Rungs 3 and 4 entirely).

The problem is not that the response is wrong. The problem is that it arrived before the other person felt received. And once a person doesn't feel received, they can't actually hear what you're saying next — because they're still trying to be heard.

Validation is the door that has to open before your partner can walk through to what you want to say. You cannot skip it. You can only either complete it or not.

What Gets in the Way of Genuine Listening

If listening were easy, everyone would do it. The fact that it's so consistently difficult — even for people who genuinely want to do it — tells you something important about what it's actually asking of you.
The most common barriers to genuine listening are not attention or effort. They are:

The Fix-It Impulse

Many people — particularly people who care deeply — respond to a partner's distress by immediately trying to solve it. This feels like love. In many relationships, it is experienced as dismissal.

"She doesn't want advice. She wants to be heard." You've probably heard some version of this before. The reason it keeps needing to be said is that the impulse to fix is genuinely hard to override, especially when you love someone and watching them in pain is uncomfortable for you too.
The fix-it impulse is not bad. It just has a timing problem. There is a moment for solutions — but it comes after the person has felt heard, not before. Offering solutions before validation is like handing someone a map before asking where they want to go.

While your partner is speaking, a voice in your head is composing a response. It's noting inaccuracies in their account, preparing corrections, building the case for your own perspective. This is not malice — it's self-protection. But it means you are not actually receiving what they're saying. You're translating it into something you can respond to.

The counter-narrative is especially active in long-running conflicts, where both partners have deeply entrenched positions. By the time your partner opens their mouth on a familiar topic, you've often already decided what they're going to say and what it means.

The Emotional Activation

When your partner's distress is directed at you, or touches something you feel defensive about, your own nervous system activates — and activated nervous systems are not good listeners. The flood of stress hormones that accompanies defensiveness, shame, or fear literally narrows your cognitive bandwidth. You can hear the words. You cannot process them fully.

This is why the Time-Out Protocol from Chapter 5 (which we will cover in detail next week) is not a listening skill — it's a precondition for listening. You cannot attune to your partner when you are flooded. The best thing you can do in that state is recognize it and ask for a pause.

📖 Jordan Learns to Listen

Jordan had always thought of himself as someone who listened. He was patient, generally. He didn't yell. He let Maya finish her sentences.

But when he did the Attunement Practice exercise from this chapter, he had to sit with something uncomfortable: he'd been processing during conversations, not receiving them. He'd been tracking what was factually accurate and what wasn't, building his rebuttal while Maya was still speaking. He'd thought this was efficient.

"Try just Rungs 1 through 3," the chapter said. "Just notice, reflect, and validate. Don't go further."

He tried it that Thursday, when Maya mentioned she'd been feeling overwhelmed with the school schedules. His instinct was to point out that he'd offered to take over the Tuesday pickups and she'd said no. Instead:

"I can see that." (Rung 1 — Notice)

"It sounds like you're really stretched thin right now." (Rung 2 — Reflect)

"That makes sense — you're managing most of the day-to-day and there's a lot of it." (Rung 3 — Validate)

Maya looked at him for a moment. "Yeah," she said. "That's exactly it."

He hadn't agreed with anything. He hadn't conceded anything. He hadn't stopped thinking his Tuesday offer had been unfairly rejected. But something in the conversation had shifted.

The Attunement Practice

This exercise is the chapter's central skill-builder. It works best when done with a specific, recent incident in mind — a conversation where your partner was upset and your response didn't land the way you would have wanted.

You're going to do two things: first, write down what you actually said or did. Then, rewrite your response using each of the five rungs of the Attunement Ladder. The goal is not to feel bad about the first version — it is to practice the second.

The Attunement Practice — Part 1

Choose a recent conversation where your partner was upset and you responded in a way you're not satisfied with. It doesn't have to be a major incident — sometimes the most useful examples are small ones.

Describe the situation briefly:

What did you actually say or do in response to your partner's distress?

What do you think your partner needed from you in that moment that they didn't get?

Now rewrite your response using the five rungs. Use the situation above. Take your time with each step — especially Rungs 3 and 4, which most people find hardest.

#	Rung	What you actually said or could have said
1	Notice	
2	Reflect	
3	Validate	
4	Empathize	
5	Respond	

The Attunement Practice — Reflection

Looking at the two versions — what you actually said, and the attunement rewrite — what's most different about them?

Which rung was hardest to write? What made it feel difficult or unnatural?

If you had responded using the ladder version in that moment, what do you think would have happened next in the conversation?

⏱ 25 minutes total	*Session time · can be split across two sittings if needed*

This is one of the most powerful sessions in the book — and one of the most difficult. It asks the listener to do something that is genuinely hard: to stay completely in receiving mode for five uninterrupted minutes.

Read the Listener Rules below before you begin. Both partners should read them. Then decide who speaks first.

☑ **Listener Rules — For the Partner Who Is Listening**

☐ No interrupting — not even to agree, not even to say "I know"

☐ No defending yourself, even if something said feels unfair or inaccurate

☐ No problem-solving — your job is not to fix what you hear

☐ No facial expressions that communicate disagreement, dismissal, or impatience

☐ When the speaker finishes: use Rungs 1–4 of the Attunement Ladder before you share your own perspective

☐ After reflecting and validating, ask: "Is there anything else?" — and genuinely wait

☐ Your response (Rung 5) comes only after the speaker says "no, that's it" or explicitly invites it

One partner speaks for five minutes about something that has been on their mind —
about themselves, their feelings, or their inner experience. This is not a complaint
session, and it is not an invitation to open a conflict. It is a chance to be heard about
something real.

Suitable topics: something you've been worrying about; something you haven't known
how to say; how you've been feeling about the relationship lately without pointing
blame; something about your own life you haven't shared enough. If you're stuck,
share how it has felt to work through the first four chapters of this workbook.

Then switch. Full cycle takes approximately 25 minutes.

If the Listener Slips

If you catch yourself interrupting, defending, or problem-solving — you don't need
to make a scene of it. Just pause, take a breath, and return to receiving mode. The
speaker can gently hold up a hand as a signal if they notice it happening. This is not a
failure. It is practice.
If emotions get intense during the exercise — for either partner — use the pause
signal from Chapter 3. Take five minutes separately. Return to the exercise. The
conversation is not over just because it got hard.

After the Listening Exercise — Debrief

Speaker: what did it feel like to be listened to in this way?

Listener: what was hardest about staying in receiving mode? What were you most
tempted to do that you didn't?

Was there a moment in the exercise where something shifted — where you felt more connected, or more understood?

What do you want to remember from this exercise and take into regular conversations?

| ⊘ 20–25 minutes total | *Session time · can be split across two sittings if needed* |

The solo work in Chapter 4 has two parts. The first is honest self-assessment of your current listening habits. The second is a practical action step you can take this week — without needing your partner to participate.

🌿 SOLO TRACK — How Do You Actually Listen?
When your partner is upset or distressed, what is your most automatic response?
Check all that apply — honestly.

☐ I try to fix the problem as quickly as possible
☐ I defend myself if the distress seems directed at me
☐ I shut down or go quiet
☐ I listen, but I'm mentally composing my response while they talk
☐ I wait for them to finish, then share my perspective
☐ I genuinely try to understand before I respond
☐ Other
☐ Other

Of the responses you checked: which one shows up most often?

What do you think drives that response — what is it protecting you from, or trying to achieve?

Is there a Rung on the Attunement Ladder that you regularly skip or struggle with? Which one, and why do you think that is?

Think of a recent conversation where your partner seemed like they weren't feeling heard. Looking back through the lens of the Attunement Ladder — what rung did you stop at? What would Rung 3 or 4 have sounded like in that conversation?

You don't need your partner's participation for this. Here's your action step for this week:

Choose one ordinary moment when your partner is talking to you about anything — it doesn't have to be heavy or emotional. Before you respond with your own thoughts, run through the first three rungs:

Rung 1 — Notice: Acknowledge what you see ("You seem stressed about that" / "I can hear that's weighing on you").
Rung 2 — Reflect: Repeat back the essence of what they said in your own words.
Rung 3 — Validate: Find the sense in their experience. "That makes sense because..."

Then — and only then — share your own perspective or ask your question.

After you've tried this at least once during the week, write about what happened:
What was the moment you tried it?

What did it feel like to do?

How did your partner respond — even if they didn't know what you were doing?

What did you notice in yourself during the attempt?

Chapter 3 asked you to change how you speak. Chapter 4 is asking something complementary and equally difficult: to change what you do while your partner is speaking.

These two chapters together form the foundation of the communication work in this book. Everything else builds on them. Conflict resolution (Chapter 5) is easier when both partners know how to open a conversation softly and receive each other's emotions without immediately defending. Intimacy (Chapter 6) deepens when both partners feel genuinely seen. Trust (Chapter 10) grows steadily in the soil of being consistently heard.

You will not do the Attunement Ladder perfectly. You will skip rungs. You will catch yourself composing your response while your partner is still talking. You will solve when they needed you to listen. This is inevitable, and it is not a problem.

What changes is the moment after you notice it. When you catch yourself doing it, you now have a choice you didn't quite have before. That's where everything starts. Being heard is one of the deepest human needs. Offering it to another person — genuinely, patiently, without requiring them to earn it first — is one of the most profound things you can do in an intimate relationship.

You're learning to do that. It doesn't happen all at once. It happens one conversation at a time.

☑ **Week 4 Closing Ritual — 5 Minutes**

☐ Share one moment this week when you felt genuinely heard — by your partner or by anyone

☐ Share one moment when you were genuinely trying to listen — and what it was like to stay in that mode

☐ Appreciation: "One thing I noticed about how you showed up this week is..."

☐ Set your session time for Week 5 — same day, same time if possible

Optional — A Moment of Being Heard

Describe a moment this week — in this workbook or outside it — when you felt truly received by another person. What made it feel that way?

⚡ 10-Minute Version — When This Is All You Have

Two things this week, in ten minutes:
1. Read the Attunement Ladder. Identify which rung you most consistently skip in difficult conversations.

2. In one conversation this week — any conversation — try Rungs 1 through 3 before you respond with your own perspective. Just once. Note what changes.

One genuine attempt at attuning — even imperfect, even small — shifts the dynamic more than a perfect conversation you never have.

A thought to carry into Week 5:
The goal of listening is not to have nothing to say. It is to make sure your partner knows they've been received before you say it. That single change — in timing, not content — transforms more conversations than almost anything else in this workbook.

Chapter 5

Fighting Differently

How to Argue Without Destroying What You're Fighting For

The goal isn't to stop fighting. The goal is to fight in a way that
makes you closer instead of further apart.

⏱ 30 minutes total	Session time · can be split across two sittings if needed

> ✂ SOLO TRACK — This chapter has its own exercises for the partner working alone. You'll find them in the Solo section below.

Conflict as Information

There is a belief that runs quietly through most relationships in distress: that conflict is a sign something is wrong. That if the relationship were healthy — if you'd chosen the right person, or were the right person — these arguments wouldn't keep happening.

This belief is wrong. And it does a lot of damage.

Conflict in a relationship is not a sign that something is broken. It is a sign that two separate human beings — with different histories, different nervous systems, different needs, different ways of understanding the world — are trying to share a life. The conflict is not the problem. The way the conflict is handled is.

Gottman's research found something that reframes everything: 69 percent of relationship conflicts are what he calls "perpetual problems" — disagreements rooted in fundamental differences of personality, values, or needs that will never be fully resolved. Not most conflicts.

Nearly all of them.

The couples who thrive are not the ones who solve these problems. They are the ones who learn to have a different relationship with them. The goal is not resolution. The goal is dialogue — the ability to revisit an ongoing disagreement with curiosity and care rather than contempt and exhaustion.

This chapter is not about teaching you to agree. It's about teaching you to fight in a way that leaves both of you feeling like you're still on the same team, even when you're at your most different.

📖 Maya and Jordan — The Dishwasher Fight (That Was Never About the Dishwasher)

They'd had the dishwasher argument seventeen times. Maya had counted.

It always started the same way: Jordan would leave dishes in the sink instead of loading them. Maya would come home to a full sink, feel the familiar tightening in her chest, and say something sharp. Jordan would feel accused, become defensive, and say something sharper. Within four minutes they were no longer talking about dishes.

They were talking about respect. About who was carrying the household. About whether Jordan saw Maya as a partner or a housekeeper. About whether Maya trusted Jordan at all. About whether they wanted the same life.

After eighteen arguments, they finally had a different conversation — not about dishes. About what each of them needed underneath the dishes fight. Maya needed to feel like the domestic load was shared. Jordan needed to feel like he wasn't walking into his own home to be corrected before he'd taken off his coat.

The dishes were never going to solve those needs. But naming the needs — for the first time, in those words — changed what the fight was actually about. And changed what was possible in it.

What the Research Shows

Gottman's longitudinal research — following couples over two decades — found that the happiest long-term couples had many of the same unresolved conflicts as couples who eventually divorced. The difference was not the problems. It was the emotional climate in which the problems lived.

Couples who stayed together and remained satisfied had developed what Gottman calls a "dialogue" with their perpetual problems — they could discuss their differences with some lightness, even humor, and without the conversation becoming a referendum on the relationship itself.

He also found that 31 percent of conflicts are "solvable problems" — situational disagreements that actually can be resolved with good communication and creative compromise. Knowing the difference between a perpetual problem and a solvable one is itself a significant step.

Most couples, when asked to describe their fights, talk about the content — who said what, who was wrong, what the issue was. But beneath the content of every conflict, there is a process: a recognizable cycle that operates the same way in almost every escalating argument, regardless of topic.

Understanding your cycle — seeing it as a pattern rather than experiencing it as an emergency — is one of the most powerful things this workbook can help you do. You can't interrupt a cycle you can't see.

The Escalation Cycle — What's Actually Happening
Most couples can recognize their own version of this pattern once they see it laid out. The key is that steps 2 and 3 — Story and Flood — happen before the argument technically begins.

1 TRIGGER	Something happens — a tone, a look, a comment, being late, being ignored. Often small. Often familiar.
↓	
2 STORY	You assign meaning: "They don't respect me." "Here we go again." "Nothing ever changes." This happens in under a second — and this is the intervention point.
↓	
3 FLOOD	Your nervous system responds to the story as if it's a physical threat. Heart rate climbs above 100 bpm. Cortisol floods in. Rational thinking degrades significantly.
↓	
4 REACTION	From a flooded state, you attack, withdraw, or shut down — the only options available when you're in survival mode. These are not chosen responses. They are physiological
↓	
5 RESPONSE	Your partner reacts to your reaction. They are now triggered. They assign their own meaning. They begin to flood. You are both now in the cycle — and the original issue is buried.

The reason the intervention point matters so much: by Step 4 (Reaction), you are already flooded. Your capacity for complex thinking, empathy, and creative problem-solving has been significantly impaired by a nervous system that believes it's under attack. You are not going to have a productive conversation from inside Step 4.

The window for changing how this goes is at Step 2 — which is why Chapter 2's work on stories was foundational. And at Step 3 — which is what the Time-Out Protocol is designed for.

You cannot think your way out of flooding. You can only wait it out, deliberately — and then return.

> On Flooding — What It Actually Feels Like
>
> Physiological flooding in conflict is often described as: heart pounding, tunnel vision, inability to think of anything except the argument, feeling like your body is in threat mode. The voice in your head becomes louder and less rational.
>
> What flooding is not: choosing to escalate. Being a bad person. Being incapable of having difficult conversations. Flooding is a biological response — the same system that protects you from physical danger, misfiring in an emotional context. It is not a character flaw. It is a nervous system doing what nervous systems do.
>
> *What this means practically: you cannot argue your way through flooding. You cannot white-knuckle your way to being reasonable while flooded. The only effective intervention is a genuine pause — long enough for the cortisol to clear.*

The Time-Out Protocol — A Pause, Not a Retreat

A structured time-out is not the same as storming out, going silent, or declaring the conversation over. It is a deliberate pause with a specific structure — one that makes it possible to return to the conversation with a nervous system that can actually participate in it.

The difference between a time-out and stonewalling comes down to one thing: the commitment to return. Stonewalling is a permanent withdrawal dressed as a pause. A time-out is a temporary withdrawal with a specific, agreed-upon structure for returning.

This is not a tool you reach for in the middle of every difficult conversation. It is specifically for moments when one or both partners is flooded — when staying in the conversation will produce more heat than light, and when the cost of continuing outweighs the cost of pausing.

THE TIME-OUT AGREEMENT

Step 1 — Either partner can call a time-out at any time — during any conversation, no matter how important. Use a neutral signal you've agreed on in advance: a word, a hand gesture, a simple "I need twenty minutes." The signal is not a criticism of your partner. It is information about your own state.

Step 2 — The time-out lasts a minimum of 20–30 minutes. During this time, do something that genuinely calms your nervous system — a walk, music, a shower, breathing exercises. Do NOT replay the argument mentally, rehearse what you'll say next, or build your case. That is not self-soothing. That is re-flooding with extra steps.

Step 3 — The partner who called the time-out is responsible for returning to the conversation. This is non-negotiable. A time-out that ends in silence is stonewalling — the Horseman from Chapter 3 — dressed in the language of self-care. Returning is the commitment that makes the time-out safe to offer.

Step 4 — When you return, begin with a repair attempt before re-entering the original topic. Don't dive straight back into the disagreement. Start with something that signals: I still want to be in relationship with you even when this is hard. Then continue the conversation.

What to Actually Do During a Time-Out

The biggest mistake people make during time-outs is using them to mentally rehearse the argument — building their case, replaying what their partner said, preparing their next move. This does not calm your nervous system. It re-floods it.

Genuine physiological calming takes about 20 minutes of actual non-conflict activity. Research suggests the most effective calming activities are:

Physical movement — a walk, stretching, light exercise. Gets the cortisol processing through your body rather than your head.

Something absorbing and neutral — music, a podcast, a task that requires just enough attention to prevent rumination.

Slow breathing — specifically extended exhales, which activate the parasympathetic nervous system.

What you should not do: scroll through social media arguments, text friends to vent about your partner, or replay the conversation in your head. These extend the flood rather than ending it.

Here is what Gottman found to be the single most reliable predictor of long-term relationship success — not communication style, not personality compatibility, not the number of conflicts. It was repair attempts.

A repair attempt is any word, gesture, or action intended to de-escalate a conflict and signal to your partner: I still want connection with you, even in this hard moment. Even this. Even now.

The crucial finding was not just about making repair attempts — it was about being able to receive them. In relationships with positive sentiment (where the underlying goodwill between partners is intact), repair attempts land. Partners recognize them, respond to them, and allow the temperature of the conflict to drop. In relationships where contempt has eroded the goodwill, repair attempts are dismissed, ignored, or interpreted as manipulation. The same words land completely differently depending on the emotional climate they're offered into.

This is why the work of earlier chapters matters here. Appreciations build goodwill. Soft startups reduce defensiveness. The Four Horsemen antidotes create a climate in which repair attempts can actually land. You've been building the conditions for this.

Repair Attempt Reference
Words and Gestures That Work

To slow things down:
"I need to slow this down."
"I'm getting overwhelmed. Can we take a minute?"
"Can we start over? I didn't mean to come out like that."

What a Repair Attempt Can Sound Like

Repair attempts don't have to be profound. They don't require eloquence or the perfect words.

They require only genuine intent — the real, in-the-moment desire to de-escalate rather than escalate.

To signal that you're still there:
"I love you even though I'm angry right now."
"I don't want to fight like this with you."
"We're on the same team. I keep forgetting that."

To acknowledge your part:
"I think I made that worse. I'm sorry."
"You're right about that part. I hear you."
"That came out wrong. Here's what I was trying to say."

Non-verbal repairs:
A hand on the arm. A moment of eye contact that says: I see you, not just this argument. A shared laugh at the absurdity of how heated it got. A brief touch that breaks the tension without resolving anything yet.

One note: a repair attempt is not a surrender, an apology for the whole argument, or a signal that you've given up your position. It's a signal that you value the relationship more than you value winning this particular exchange.

📖 Maya and Jordan — The First Repair

It happened three weeks after they'd started the workbook. Not planned. Not practiced. Jordan had come home late again, and Maya had said something that had an edge in it — not the Soft Startup version, the old version.

Jordan had gone quiet. Maya had recognized the shutdown coming, the familiar wall, and something shifted in her before she could think it through: she didn't want to be in the old cycle again.

She said: "I don't want to do this fight again. I'm tired of it. I love you."

Jordan looked up from his phone.

"I'm tired of it too," he said.

Neither of them said much for a while after that. They sat on the couch and watched something on television and occasionally commented on it. It wasn't a resolved argument. It wasn't a breakthrough. It was a repair — small, imperfect, enough.

The next day, Maya came back to the conversation. Calm this time. Using the Soft Startup. "I felt hurt last night when..." Jordan listened using the framework from Chapter 4. They talked for twenty minutes and didn't resolve anything permanently — but they understood each other better. And that was enough to begin again.

Perpetual Problems vs. Solvable Problems — Knowing the Difference

Not all conflicts are the same, and treating them the same way wastes a lot of relational energy.

Solvable problems are situational. They have a specific context, a concrete behavior at the center, and some form of resolution available if both partners are willing to negotiate. Who handles drop-off on Thursdays. Whether to spend Christmas with your family or theirs this year. How to handle the credit card debt. These are real and sometimes painful conversations — but they have solutions.

Perpetual problems are different. They are rooted in enduring differences in personality, values, needs, or worldview. One partner needs more alone time; the other needs more togetherness. One is a spender; the other is a saver. One is spontaneous; the other craves structure. These differences are not flaws to be corrected. They are the actual differences between two people who are not the same person.

Here is the mistake most couples make: they treat perpetual problems like solvable ones. They keep trying to resolve them — to reach a final answer that will settle the question permanently. This strategy fails, repeatedly, and produces the experience of having the same argument seventeen times. The argument about dishes was really about fairness and feeling seen — and those are not dishwasher problems. They are perpetual-problem territory.

SOLVABLE PROBLEMS	PERPETUAL PROBLEMS
• Situational — has a specific context • A resolution exists with enough goodwill • Goal: negotiate a specific solution *Examples: who handles which chores; holiday scheduling; a financial decision; a one-time disagreement about how to handle a situation*	• Rooted in enduring personality/value differences • No permanent resolution — requires ongoing dialogue • Goal: understand each other's positions; coexist with the difference *Examples: different needs for alone time vs. togetherness; different spending styles; different parenting philosophies; different social needs*

How to Tell Which Type You're Dealing With

Ask yourself: Has this argument come up before, roughly in the same form? If yes — and especially if the same positions emerge each time — it's likely perpetual. The goal shifts from "how do we solve this" to "how do we understand each other's position and find a way to live with the difference."

If the conflict is genuinely situational — it hasn't come up before, it has a specific context, a concrete decision point — the goal is negotiation. The Soft Startup, the Listener's Framework, and a genuine willingness to find a middle ground are the tools for this.

Most couples who are stuck have misidentified perpetual problems as solvable ones — and keep trying to solve what can only be accepted, managed, and dialogued with. Recognising which type you're dealing with is itself a significant step.

Before the Together and Solo sessions this week, take time to map your own conflict pattern. This is best done individually — your maps will likely differ, and the difference is itself useful information.

Our Conflict Map — Complete Individually, Then Compare

Think about the conflict that comes up most often between you and your partner. Answer these questions from your own perspective.

What usually triggers this conflict? (The observable event — a behavior, a tone, a situation)

What story do you immediately tell yourself when you're triggered? (From Chapter 2 — what meaning do you assign?)

How do you know when you're flooding? What does it feel like in your body?

What do you do when you're flooded — attack, withdraw, or shut down? Be specific.

How does the conflict typically end — is it resolved, dropped, or left unfinished?

Is this a solvable problem or a perpetual one? (Your honest assessment)

What repair attempt could you offer that would feel genuine — during this conflict, or the next time it starts?

What repair attempt from your partner would mean the most to you to receive?

Your Time-Out Agreement — Write It Together or Solo

Before you need a time-out in a real conflict, agree on the specifics. Vague agreements fail at the worst moments.

Our time-out signal will be: (a word, a phrase, a gesture — something neutral and agreed-upon)

Our time-out minimum duration will be: (research suggests 20–30 minutes as a minimum)

The partner who calls the time-out commits to: (returning to the conversation, signaling when they're ready)

What we will each do during a time-out to genuinely calm down: (be specific — not "think about it")

<table>
<tr><td>⏱ 25 minutes total</td><td>Session time · can be split across two sittings if needed</td></tr>
</table>

This session uses a recurring conflict as material — not to resolve it, but to understand it differently than you have before. Choose a conflict that comes up regularly. Not your most explosive one. Something real, but not at the edge of what the relationship can hold right now.

💬 The Structured Conflict Conversation

Part 1 — Each partner describes their experience of the conflict (5 minutes each):
One partner speaks while the other uses the Listener's Framework from Chapter 4: reflect, validate, then respond. No debating the accuracy of each other's experience. The goal is to genuinely understand how the conflict feels from the inside for each of you.

Part 2 — Each partner names the need or fear underneath their position (5 minutes each):
Use this sentence: "When this conflict happens, what I'm really needing is _____" or "When this conflict happens, what I'm afraid of is _____."
Often the actual need — the thing underneath the position — is not what the argument appears to be about. Jordan's position about the dishes was not really about the dishes. Maya's need was not to have a cleaner sink. Finding the need underneath is the work.

Part 3 — Together: identify one small shift (5 minutes):
Not a solution to the perpetual problem — a small, specific shift that would make this conflict feel less like war and more like a hard conversation. Something one or both of you could try before the next time this comes up.
Write it down. Vague intentions evaporate. Concrete ones don't.

What did you learn about how your partner experiences this conflict — something you didn't fully understand before?

What was the need or fear underneath your own position? Did naming it feel different from the usual argument?

The one small shift we agreed to try:

Solo Track — For the Partner Working Alone

◑ 20–25 minutes total	*Session time · can be split across two sittings if needed*

The solo work in Chapter 5 focuses on two things: understanding your own role in the conflict cycle more deeply, and building a repair practice you can deploy regardless of whether your partner is engaging with the workbook.

🌿 SOLO TRACK — Understanding Your Part of the Cycle

Think about the conflict that comes up most often between you and your partner. Work through these questions honestly — this is solo reflection, so there's no one to manage your answers for.

At what point in the escalation cycle do you usually take the conflict to the next level? (The trigger, the story, the flood, the reaction?)

What does your flooding feel like? What are the physical signs that you're no longer in a place to have a productive conversation?

What do you typically do when flooded — and what does that do to your partner?

Has this conflict been a solvable problem that you've been treating as perpetual — or a perpetual problem you've been trying to solve? What would change if you correctly identified it?

Repair attempts work best when they're genuine — not scripted, not performed, but real. Here's a way to build your own.

List three things you could genuinely say or do this week that would de-escalate tension between you and your partner — whether during a conflict or entirely outside of one. Be specific:

1.____
____
____
2.____
____
____
3.____
____
____

Choose one of the three above. This week — not in a manufactured moment, but when an opportunity arises naturally — offer it.

Note what happened (even if the outcome was uncertain or imperfect):

A note specifically for the solo reader: repair attempts work even when your partner doesn't know you're making one. A moment of warmth, a genuine gesture, a comment that signals goodwill rather than grievance — these shift the emotional climate of a relationship whether or not they're acknowledged. You are not powerless here.

The three weeks of the Communication section of this workbook have built toward this: the possibility of a different kind of fight.

Not a fight that's free of pain, or frustration, or genuine disagreement. But a fight that both people can survive — that leaves you feeling like you've been in the presence of each other rather than at war with each other, even when the issue isn't resolved.

This requires three things that are hard to hold simultaneously: the capacity to name your own experience clearly (the Soft Startup), the capacity to genuinely hear your partner's experience without defending against it (the Listener's Framework), and the capacity to interrupt the escalation cycle before it becomes destructive (the time-out, the repair attempt).

None of these things will work perfectly the first time. Many of them will fail in the heat of a real conflict, especially early on. The question is not whether you execute them flawlessly. The question is whether you begin to believe that a different kind of fight is actually possible — and whether you keep reaching for the tools even when you miss.

Gottman's research on repair attempts found something that is quietly one of the most hopeful findings in relationship science: the repair attempt doesn't have to be accepted to matter. Making the attempt — reaching toward your partner even when you're still angry, even when the words come out imperfectly — shifts something in the relationship, whether or not the gesture lands cleanly.

You are practicing something real. It will get easier. Keep going.

Week 5 is the last chapter of Part Two — Communication. Next week, the book shifts into Part Three: Connection. The closing ritual this week is worth doing carefully. You've covered a lot of ground.

☑ Week 5 Closing Ritual — 5 Minutes
□ Share one moment this week you handled a conflict differently than usual — even a small difference counts
□ Name one repair attempt you made or received this week, however imperfect
□ Review and confirm your Time-Out Agreement — make sure you both know the signal and the terms
□ Appreciation: tell your partner one specific thing about how they showed up this week that you noticed

---

Looking Back on Part Two — A Brief Reflection
We've now completed three weeks on communication — Chapters 3, 4, and 5. Before moving into Part Three, take a moment to notice:

What has shifted in how you communicate, even slightly, since Chapter 3?

What skill from the Communication section do you most want to keep practicing?

Two things, in ten minutes:
1. Map your own conflict cycle on paper — trigger, story, flood, reaction, response. Just your side.
2. Write your Time-Out Agreement — the signal, the duration, the return commitment.
Having the agreement before you need it is the entire point. Ten minutes now prevents forty minutes of damage later.

A thought to carry into Part Three:
You've spent three weeks learning to speak more carefully, listen more fully, and fight without destroying what you're fighting for. The next three weeks are about something different — about finding your way back to the person you chose, and the life you're building together.

Chapter 6

Your Partner Is A Stranger

Rebuilding Emotional Intimacy and Genuine Curiosity

You may know everything about your partner's schedule and almost nothing about their inner world. This chapter is about the difference — and about becoming curious again.

○30 minutes total	*Session time · can be split across two sittings if needed*

🌿 SOLO TRACK — This chapter has its own exercises for the partner working alone. You'll find them in the Solo section below.

The Problem With Assuming You Know

There is a particular loneliness that lives inside long-term relationships — the loneliness of being with someone who has stopped being curious about you.

Not someone who has stopped loving you. Not someone who has stopped trying. Someone who simply believes they already know you. Who fills in your thoughts before you finish saying them. Who predicts your reaction before you have one. Who has stopped asking, because they've decided they already know.

This is one of the most common — and most quietly damaging — forms of relational drift. It doesn't announce itself. It accumulates over years of familiarity until the two of you have stopped discovering each other and started maintaining a static portrait of who the other person was, the last time you were really paying attention.

Gottman calls the mental model each partner holds of the other's inner world a "Love Map" — a detailed, continuously updated knowledge of who your partner is: their fears, their dreams, their embarrassments, their sources of joy, their current stresses, their unspoken needs. In the early stages of a relationship, these maps are constantly updated. We're hungry to know this person. We ask questions. We're surprised by the answers. We update the map.

Over time, most couples stop updating. They assume the map is complete. They navigate by an old version — sometimes years out of date — and then wonder why they keep feeling lost.

This chapter is about picking up the pen again.

📖 Maya and Jordan — The Question She'd Stopped Asking

They were washing up after dinner — Phoebe in bed, the house quiet for once — and Jordan said something offhand about a colleague who was leaving the firm to start something of his own.

Maya said, "Hm," and handed him a plate to dry.

What she didn't say — what she'd stopped asking, somewhere in the last three years — was: "Does that ever make you think about what you'd do, if you could start something?" She'd assumed she already knew the answer. Jordan was steady, cautious, good at his job, not a risk-taker. She'd filed that under "who Jordan is" and stopped checking.

She would have been wrong. Jordan had been quietly researching franchise ownership for eighteen months. He'd never mentioned it because he assumed Maya would dismiss it as impractical — which was his filed version of who she was, the map he'd stopped updating too.

Two people in the same kitchen, each holding an outdated portrait of the other, passing plates in silence.

This is what happens when couples stop being curious. Not dramatically. Just quietly, over time, until the relationship runs on assumption rather than discovery.

What Genuine Curiosity Actually Does

In 1997, psychologist Arthur Aron published a study that became one of the most cited — and most misunderstood — pieces of relationship research of the last thirty years. He brought pairs of strangers together and had them ask each other thirty-six questions, progressively more intimate, over the course of ninety minutes.

Several of those pairs fell in love.

The popular interpretation of this study is that the questions were some kind of magic — that vulnerability-inducing questions create connection. But that's not quite what the research shows. The mechanism was more specific: it was structured mutual disclosure matched with structured mutual curiosity. Both people answering honestly. Both people listening genuinely. Both people being surprised by what they heard.

That combination — honest self-disclosure received with genuine curiosity — is what creates intimacy. Not the questions themselves. The questions were just a delivery system for something that the two strangers in the study had, which many long-term couples have gradually lost: the experience of genuinely not knowing what the other person was going to say.

The antidote to the stale Love Map is not grand romantic gestures. It's not a weekend away. It's the simple, disciplined practice of asking your partner questions you don't already know the answers to — and being genuinely interested in what you hear.

Most couples need this more urgently than they need better conflict resolution. Before you can fight well together, you need to actually know each other again. Before you can rebuild intimacy, you need to feel curious again. Curiosity is the emotion that intimacy runs on.

What the Research Shows

Gottman's research identified what he calls "Love Map" strength as one of the foundational components of relationship health. Couples with rich, frequently updated Love Maps showed significantly higher relationship satisfaction, were better able to navigate conflict without it becoming permanently damaging, and reported greater overall friendship and fondness for their partner.

He also found that Love Maps erode predictably under stress — when life becomes demanding and couples focus on logistics rather than connection, the inner worlds of both partners drift out of view. Rebuilding them is not complicated. It requires only two things: questions that go beyond logistics, and answers that go beyond the expected.

The couples who sustain intimacy over decades are not, Gottman found, the ones who feel the most passion. They are the ones who remain genuinely interested in each other — who treat each other as ongoing sources of discovery rather than settled quantities.

The Love Map Update — Ten Questions Each

The questions below are designed to update your Love Map — to access parts of your partner's inner world that daily life rarely reaches. They're not conversation starters for dinner parties. They're invitations to places you may not have been in each other for a while.

Instructions: each partner answers all ten questions independently, in writing, before sharing. Write what's actually true — not what you think sounds interesting, and not the version you assume your partner wants to hear. The purpose of the exercise is to be known, and you can only be known if you're honest.

After you've both written your answers, share them — question by question, or in whatever order feels right. As you share, the listener's only job is to be curious. Ask follow-up questions. Be surprised. Resist the urge to jump ahead to your own answer or to already know what your partner is going to say.

Answer on your own first. Write what's genuinely true — not what sounds good.
1. What is one thing I am genuinely worried about right now that I haven't told you?

2. What is something I'm quietly proud of that I've never really said out loud?

3. When do I feel most like myself?

4. What is one dream I've quietly let go of in the last five years?

5. What do I most need from you right now — that I don't know how to ask for?

6. What part of my day do I find most draining, and why?

7. What do I find myself thinking about before I fall asleep?

8. What do I miss about us, from an earlier time?

9. What am I most afraid of — about this relationship, or about life in general?

10. What would I do differently if I weren't afraid of failing?

Answer on your own first. Write what's genuinely true — not what sounds good.

1. What is one thing I am genuinely worried about right now that I haven't told you?

2. What is something I'm quietly proud of that I've never really said out loud?

3. When do I feel most like myself?

4. What is one dream I've quietly let go of in the last five years?

5. What do I most need from you right now — that I don't know how to ask for?

6. What part of my day do I find most draining, and why?

7. What do I find myself thinking about before I fall asleep?

8. What do I miss about us, from an earlier time?

9. What am I most afraid of — about this relationship, or about life in general?

10. What would I do differently if I weren't afraid of failing?

After You Share — Listener's Only Job

When your partner shares their answers, your only job is to be curious.

This means:

Ask follow-up questions: "Tell me more about that." "When did you start feeling that way?" "What does that feel like?"

Be genuinely surprised: If you weren't surprised by a single answer, ask yourself if you were really listening — or if you were filtering what you heard through the map you already had.

Don't fix, advise, or reassure: Not yet. This is a discovery exercise, not a problem-solving session. If something your partner shares needs a response, give it space — come back to it after the full sharing.

The goal is not to agree with everything you hear. It is to understand it. Understanding comes before response. Always.

After Sharing — What You Learned

What answer from your partner surprised you most?

Was there an answer you gave that surprised you — something you didn't fully know until you wrote it down?

What is one thing you want to know more about — something their answer opened that you'd like to explore further?

Bids for Connection — The Currency of Intimacy

The Love Map Update is a structured exercise. But most of the connection in a long-term relationship doesn't happen in structured exercises. It happens in the ordinary, unremarkable moments of a shared life — moments so small that most couples have stopped noticing them entirely.

Gottman calls these moments "bids for connection." A bid is any attempt — however small, however unspectacular — to connect with your partner. It can be a comment: "

Look at this." "That's interesting." "Can you believe this?" It can be a gesture: a hand on the shoulder, a smile across the kitchen, a touch as you pass in the hallway. It can be a question: "How was your call?" "How are you feeling?"

These bids are so ordinary that they're easy to dismiss as inconsequential. They are not. They are the fundamental unit of connection in a relationship. And research shows that how partners respond to these small, daily bids is one of the most reliable predictors of whether the relationship will survive and whether it will feel good to be in.

Partners respond to bids in one of three ways:

Turning Toward

Acknowledging the bid, engaging with it, receiving it. "Look at this" gets a look. "That's interesting" gets genuine attention. A shoulder touch gets a lean-in. This doesn't have to be elaborate. It has to be present.

Turning Away

Ignoring the bid, missing it, being too absorbed in something else to register it. This is usually not hostile — it's distracted. But from the perspective of the person who made the bid, distraction and dismissal feel nearly identical. The bid went unmet.

Turning Against

Criticizing or dismissing the bid. "You always interrupt me with things like that." "Why would I care about that?" This is the most damaging response — it doesn't just leave the bid unmet, it communicates that bidding itself was a mistake.

What the Research Shows

Gottman's longitudinal research found that couples who remained together and happy over time turned toward each other's bids an average of 86% of the time. Couples who divorced turned toward each other's bids an average of 33% of the time. This wasn't measured during conflicts or hard conversations. It was measured in ordinary moments — at breakfast, watching television, doing dishes.

The implication is significant: the health of a relationship is not primarily built in the big conversations. It is built in the hundred small moments every day when a bid is made and either received or missed.

What this means practically: you don't have to have a perfect conversation this week. You have to turn toward your partner more often in the moments that don't feel like conversations at all.

The Bid Awareness Practice runs over three days. Use the tracker below to capture what you notice.

☑ Bid Awareness Practice — Three Days
☐ Day 1: Observe — count the bids your partner makes without changing your behavior. Just notice.

☐ Day 1: Track — how often did you turn toward versus turn away? Use the tracker below.

☐ Day 2: Increase — intentionally turn toward your partner's bids 10% more than usual. No announcement.

☐ Day 3: Notice — has anything shifted in the feeling between you? What do you observe?

Day	Turned Toward (✓)	Turned Away (✗)	What I noticed
Day 1 — Observe			
Day 2 — Increase by 10%			
Day 3 — Notice the shift			

After three days of paying attention: what surprised you about how often your partner bids for connection?

Which bid type do you most often miss — and why do you think that is?

When you intentionally increased your turning-toward responses on Day 2, what happened to the atmosphere between you?

What Curiosity Looks Like in Daily Life

The Love Map Update and the Bid Awareness Practice are exercises. But the goal of Chapter 6 is not to have you do exercises. The goal is to change the posture you bring to your partner on an ordinary Tuesday.

Curiosity, as a relational posture, means treating your partner as someone you are still learning about — rather than someone you have already figured out. It means asking questions to which you do not already know the answer. It means being genuinely open to being surprised.

In practice, this looks like small things:

It looks like asking "what's been on your mind lately?" instead of "how was your day?" — because one question invites inner world access and the other invites a logistics report.

It looks like following up on things your partner mentioned last week: "Did that meeting ever happen? How did it go?" Demonstrating that you were actually listening, and that you remembered, is one of the most quietly powerful things you can do in a relationship.

It looks like noticing when your partner seems different — quieter, more animated, more tired — and asking about it rather than waiting for them to volunteer. "You seem like something's on your mind. Is there?"

None of these things take more than sixty seconds. All of them update the Love Map. All of them tell your partner: I am still paying attention to you. I am still curious about who you are. I have not decided you are finished.

📖 **Maya and Jordan — The Question She Finally Asked**
It was a Wednesday evening, dishes done, Phoebe in bed. Maya had been thinking about the workbook exercise all day.
She sat down next to Jordan on the couch and said: "Can I ask you something real?"
Jordan muted the television. "Sure."
"What's something you've been thinking about that you haven't told me?"
A beat of silence. Then: "Honestly?" He looked at her. "I've been thinking about leaving the firm."
Maya stared at him. "To do what?"
"I don't know exactly. Something smaller. Something where I actually know the people I work with." He paused. "I've been researching franchise opportunities. Just looking. I probably wouldn't—"
"How long have you been thinking about this?"
"A year and a half, maybe."
A year and a half. She'd been living with a person who'd been quietly carrying something for eighteen months and she hadn't known. Because she'd assumed she already knew who he was.
She didn't have an answer for him. She didn't offer an opinion. She just said: "Tell

⏱ **25 minutes** total +1 connection date this week	*Session time · can be split across two sittings if needed*

This week's Together Track has two parts — one for your session, and one for later in the week.

Using the Love Map Update questions above: each partner shares answers to at least three of the ten questions — the three that feel most true or most alive right now. As you share, the listener practices the posture of genuine curiosity from Chapter 4: notice, reflect, validate, and ask follow-up questions rather than jumping to your own response.

The session is not a debate. If your partner's answer surprises you, let it surprise you. If it raises something difficult, note it — you can return to it another time. The purpose of this session is discovery, not resolution.

Part 2 — The Connection Date

Before next week, schedule one connection date. This does not have to be elaborate or expensive. It can be forty-five minutes at the kitchen table after Phoebe is in bed, phones in another room, doing nothing except talking to each other.

The rules for the connection date are simple:

Connection Date — The Only Rules

Phones away. Not on the table. Not face-down. In another room.

No logistics. No discussing schedules, bills, school events, or things that need to be organised. Those conversations exist. This one doesn't.

Use the Love Map questions if you're stuck. Any of the ten work. Or make your own. Or simply ask: "What's something I don't know about you right now?"

Stay curious. If something your partner says is surprising, interesting, or even difficult — stay in it. Ask a follow-up question before moving on.

After the Session and the Date

What was one answer from your partner — in the session or on the date — that you want to remember?

Was there a moment when you felt genuinely curious about your partner — the way you did early in the relationship?

What is one thing you learned about your partner this week that you didn't know (or had forgotten)?

<table>
<tr><td>⏱ 20–25 minutes total</td><td>Session time · can be split across two sittings if needed</td></tr>
</table>

The solo work in Chapter 6 has two parts. The first is the Love Map exercise done on your own. The second is an action step you can take this week without your partner's awareness or participation.

🌿 SOLO TRACK — Your Love Map — Solo Version
Complete the ten Love Map questions for yourself — answering honestly, not performing. Then answer these additional questions.

Looking at your ten answers: which one surprised you? Which one felt most important to say out loud, even if only on paper?

Looking at your ten answers: which one surprised you? Which one felt most important to say out loud, even if only on paper?

Now think about your partner. Of the ten questions, which one do you most want to know their answer to? Why that one?

If you had to guess your partner's answer to question 5 ("What do I most need from you right now, that I don't know how to ask for?") — what would you guess? What does that guess tell you?

When did you last ask your partner a question that genuinely surprised you with its answer? What was the question?

This week, ask your partner one genuine question that you don't already know the answer to — not a logistics question, but a real question about their inner world.

Write the question you plan to ask before you ask it:

You can ask it anywhere — at dinner, on a walk, in the car. You don't need to explain why you're asking. You can simply ask.

After you've asked it, write what happened:
Did they seem surprised by the question?

Did they open up — or deflect?

Did you learn something you didn't know?

What did it feel like — for you — to ask a genuine question and wait for a genuine answer?

What This Week Is Really About

Part Three of this workbook — Connection — begins here. And it begins with something that looks simple and is quietly one of the most challenging things a long-term couple can attempt: to see each other freshly.

Familiarity is one of the great gifts of a long relationship. It is also one of its great hazards. The same familiarity that makes you comfortable with each other can make you invisible to each other — known in the administrative sense, unknown in the human one.

The couples who sustain genuine intimacy over decades are not the ones who never drift. They are the ones who notice the drift and do something about it. Who pick up the pen and update the map. Who ask the question they've been assuming they know the answer to. Who schedule the forty-five minutes even when the week is full

Curiosity is not something you either have or don't have about your partner. It's something you choose or don't choose, every day, in the small moments when a bid is made and you either turn toward it or away. In the quiet evenings when you either ask a real question or scroll your phone instead.

Chapters 6, 7, and 8 are about rebuilding connection — emotional, physical, and relational. They work best in sequence, but they work only if you bring the same attention to them that you brought to the communication chapters. The skills you learned in Chapters 3 and 4 are the tools. The curiosity you're practicing now is the fuel.

☑ **Week 6 Closing Ritual — 5 Minutes**
□ Share one thing you learned about your partner this week that you didn't know or had forgotten
□ Name one bid for connection you made this week — and how it was received
□ Confirm your connection date if it hasn't happened yet — agree on when
□ Appreciation: "One thing I love about who you are is..." — be specific

⚡ **10-Minute Version — When This Is All You Have**
Two things, in ten minutes:
1. Each partner answers three Love Map questions independently — choose whichever three feel most alive.
2. Share one answer each. The listener asks one follow-up question before responding.
Three questions, two partners, one follow-up question each. Ten minutes. Something will shift.

A thought to carry into Week 7:
You did not stop being interesting when you became familiar. Your partner did not stop surprising you because they ran out of surprises. You stopped asking. This week, you started again. That's not a small thing.

Chapter 7

The Missing Language of Touch

Rebuilding Physical and Sensory Intimacy

Physical intimacy doesn't begin in the bedroom. It begins with ten thousand small moments of touch, presence, and attention that most couples have quietly stopped noticing.

⏱30 minutes total	Session time · can be split across two sittings if needed

🔖 SOLO TRACK — This chapter has its own exercises for the partner working alone. You'll find them in the Solo section below.

How Physical Distance Happens

Physical disconnection in a long-term relationship almost never arrives all at once. There is no moment when a couple decides to become touch-distant. It happens the same way emotional drift happens: gradually, incrementally, through small abandonments that each feel too minor to address.

The goodbye kiss that became a forehead peck, then a wave from the door, then nothing. The hand-holding that stopped sometime after the stroller arrived — hands too full, pace too different. The spontaneous hug after a long day that became a nod from the kitchen doorway because someone needed to start dinner and someone else needed to check the phone. The moment in bed when reaching over stopped feeling like an invitation and started feeling like an obligation, and then stopped happening at all.

None of these moments were decisions. They were the path of least resistance, chosen again and again until the path hardened into a road and the road hardened into the only way things are.

What makes physical distance particularly painful is that it is experienced differently by different people. For many people, physical touch is not a luxury or a preference — it is one of the primary languages through which they receive love and feel safe in a relationship. When that language goes quiet, they don't just feel less connected. They feel less loved, less wanted, and less secure — even if nothing else in the relationship has changed.

Understanding why physical distance happens — and what it means to each partner — is the first step toward moving back toward each other.

It hadn't always been like this. Maya could remember, precisely, what it had felt like in the beginning: Jordan's hand finding hers in a cinema before the lights went down. The way he'd put a hand on the small of her back when they were standing in a group. The morning ritual of lying close before either of them got up.

She couldn't say exactly when those things had stopped. She knew that somewhere in the years of Phoebe's infancy — the exhaustion, the broken nights, the sense that her body was no longer quite her own — she'd stopped being available in ways she used to be. Jordan had stopped reaching, maybe because she'd turned away enough times that reaching felt like risk.

Now they slept on their respective sides of the bed, a foot of space between them that neither of them talked about.

What Maya hadn't told Jordan — what she'd been carrying without fully knowing she was carrying it — was that she missed him. Not the complicated, difficult version of their relationship that required workbooks and conversations and careful sentence frames. She missed his hand on her shoulder. She missed feeling held.

The physical distance wasn't a symptom of not loving each other. It was a symptom of two people who'd stopped knowing how to get back across the space that had grown between them.

What Physical Touch Actually Does

The research on physical affection in long-term relationships is among the most consistent in the field: non-sexual physical touch — holding hands, hugging, sitting close, a hand on the back, a touch on the arm — is one of the strongest predictors of relationship satisfaction over time, and one of the first things to erode when a relationship is under strain.

This is not simply about comfort or sentiment. There are measurable physiological mechanisms at work. Physical touch between partners triggers the release of oxytocin — the hormone associated with bonding and trust — and reduces cortisol, the primary stress hormone. Couples who maintain regular physical affection report lower levels of chronic stress, higher immune function, and significantly greater relationship satisfaction than those who don't, even after controlling for other factors.

What this means practically: physical affection is not just the expression of a healthy relationship. It is one of the inputs that keeps a relationship healthy. It's not only something you do when things are good. It's something you do to help things be good.

This cuts against the intuition many couples have when they're struggling: that physical closeness should wait until things feel better emotionally. For many couples, it works the other way around. Small, consistent acts of non-sexual physical affection — initiated even when things feel distant — can shift the emotional temperature of a relationship more quickly than almost any conversation.

A 2014 study by Debrot and colleagues found that physical affection between partners mediates the relationship between positive emotions and relationship satisfaction — meaning touch is part of the mechanism by which positive feelings translate into relationship wellbeing, not just a downstream effect of it.

Gottman's research identifies what he calls "the six-second kiss" as one of his simplest and most reliably effective interventions: a real, intentional, non-perfunctory kiss lasting at least six seconds, practiced daily. Couples who introduce this single ritual consistently report measurable increases in feelings of connection, warmth, and relationship satisfaction within weeks.

Six seconds. That is less time than it takes to read this paragraph. And the research says it moves the needle.

Desire Discrepancy — The Conversation Most Couples Avoid

Non-sexual affection is one conversation. Sexual intimacy is another — and for most couples, a significantly harder one to have.

Desire discrepancy — a mismatch between partners in their level of interest in sexual intimacy — is one of the most common features of long-term relationships and one of the least discussed. Research from Emily Nagoski's work on sexuality and desire, as well as broader studies on long-term couples, suggests that some degree of desire discrepancy is present in the majority of committed relationships, and is not, in itself, a sign that something is wrong.

What determines whether desire discrepancy becomes a problem is not its existence but how couples handle it. When it goes undiscussed — when one partner silently interprets their partner's lower desire as rejection, or when the higher-desire partner feels perpetually guilty for wanting — the silence calcifies into distance and sometimes into damage.

There are many factors that shift desire over the course of a long relationship: stress, parenting demands, hormonal changes, mental health, body image, the emotional temperature of the relationship itself, medication, illness, and the simple accumulation of years during which both people have changed. None of these factors are moral failures. Most of them are not permanent. All of them are worth understanding rather than avoiding.

This chapter will not tell you what your sexual relationship should look like. That is yours to determine, together, with honesty and care. What it will do is give you a structured way to begin the conversation — one that reduces the likelihood of shame, blame, or defensiveness hijacking what is, at its core, a conversation about wanting to feel close to each other.

> Important Note on This Chapter
> If the decline in physical or sexual intimacy in your relationship is significantly affecting your wellbeing, your sense of self, or your sense of the relationship's viability, this chapter provides a starting framework — but the conversation it opens often benefits from the support of a therapist or, for sexual concerns specifically, a sex therapist.
>
> There is no shame in needing more help with this topic than a workbook can offer. Some of these conversations have roots that go deeper than exercises can reach. Knowing when to bring in professional support is itself a form of taking care of the relationship.
>
> *If you are in the Together Track and your partner is not ready to engage with the sexual intimacy portion of this chapter, work only with the non-sexual affection sections for now. The door to the harder conversation will be easier to open once more physical warmth has been restored.*

The Physical Intimacy Check-In

Complete this independently before sharing with your partner. Answer each section honestly — not diplomatically, not with your partner's reaction in mind, but with what is genuinely true for you right now.

The four areas in the table below cover the full range of physical connection in a relationship — from the small daily gestures to the deeper intimacy conversation. Score each area from 1 (very low satisfaction) to 10 (very strong satisfaction), then use the notes column to capture what's changed, what you miss, or what you most want more of.

Score each area 1–10 and note what's changed or what you most want. Complete before comparing with your partner.

Area	Score 1–10	What's changed / what I most want
Non-sexual physical affection *Hugs, hand-holding, casual touch, sitting close*	——	
Emotional intimacy through physical presence *Feeling seen and held without words*	——	
Intentional physical rituals *Greetings, goodbyes, bedtime routines*	——	
Sexual intimacy *Frequency, quality, feeling desired, feeling safe*	——	

After Scoring — What This Tells Me

Which area scored lowest for you — and what do you think is driving that?

Is there something you have been wanting to say to your partner about physical connection that you haven't found the right way to say?

What would feel like a meaningful, manageable step toward more physical connection this week — something that doesn't require a perfect conversation first?

Gottman's six-second kiss intervention sounds, the first time you hear it, almost absurdly simple. Kiss your partner for six seconds every day. Not a peck — a real kiss, with intention and presence, long enough that you both have to stop whatever else you're doing.

Six seconds is longer than you think. Try counting it out right now. That pause — that requirement to be actually present with your partner for six uninterrupted seconds — is precisely what makes it work. You cannot have a six-second kiss while checking your phone. You cannot have a six-second kiss while distracted, or hurried, or resentful. To do it genuinely requires a moment of choosing your partner. And choosing your partner, again and again in small ways, is how connection is built and rebuilt.

The six-second kiss is one example of what researchers call a "transitional ritual" — a physical act that marks the beginning or end of a shared time together and anchors both partners in the relationship. Other examples: a real hug when one partner returns home (thirty seconds or more, long enough for nervous systems to sync). A hand held for a few minutes in bed before sleep. A shoulder touch when passing in the kitchen. A forehead kiss at departure.

These rituals don't require a repaired relationship to begin. They can be the beginning of the repair themselves. The physical gesture often creates the emotional opening, rather than waiting for the emotional opening to create the physical gesture.

This is counter-intuitive for many couples, who feel that physical closeness should wait until emotional closeness is restored. The research consistently suggests the opposite is often true: physical touch, offered gently and consistently, creates the safety in which emotional repair becomes possible.

> **The Six-Second Kiss — How to Introduce It**
>
> You don't need a formal conversation to begin this ritual. You can simply do it — once, today, and see what happens. If your partner seems surprised or confused, you can say: "I read something that said we should try this. Six seconds. Can we?" If your relationship is in a place where spontaneous physical contact feels fraught, you can raise it explicitly during the Together Track session: "I want to try introducing one small physical ritual. Can we agree to a six-second kiss once a day this week?"
>
> *The ritual only needs to happen once a day. It only needs to last six seconds. Start there. Adjust from there.*

> **⊙ 20 minutes total** — *Session time · can be split across two sittings if needed*

This session has a clear structure and a clear purpose: to share what you each completed in the Physical Intimacy Check-In, and to agree on two specific physical rituals to introduce this week.

Read the guidelines below before you begin. The physical intimacy conversation is one of the most emotionally charged conversations this workbook asks you to have. The skills from Chapters 3 and 4 — soft startup, listening before responding, validation before reaction — matter here more than almost anywhere else.

How to Share the Check-In — Guidelines

Each partner shares their completed Check-In scores and notes — one area at a time. The listener uses the Attunement Ladder from Chapter 4: notice, reflect, validate, and empathize before sharing their own perspective.

If a score surprises you: don't challenge it. Receive it. Ask: "Tell me more about what's behind that score." Curiosity first, response second.

If something your partner shares is difficult to hear: take a breath before responding. Remind yourself that what they are describing is their experience — not an accusation, not a verdict, not something they are doing to you.

If the sexual intimacy section feels too raw to discuss right now: name that explicitly. "I'm not ready to talk about that part yet. Can we focus on the non-sexual sections for now?" That is a complete and honorable answer.

The goal of this conversation is not resolution. It is mutual understanding of where each of you actually is. That understanding is enough for this week.

After sharing your Check-Ins, use the Rituals Agreement table below to agree on two or three specific physical rituals to introduce this week. Be concrete — vague intentions don't become habits. Name the what, and name the when.

Ritual type	What we're committing to	When / how often
Non-sexual ritual	*e.g. a 20-second hug, 30-second hug of non-demanding, hand-holding while watching tv*	
Presence ritual	*e.g. five minutes of genuine check-in before phones at end of day*	
Towards closeness	*Something that moves gently in the direction of the intimacy conversation you had*	

After the Session — What We Noticed

What was it like to share your Physical Intimacy Check-In with your partner?

Was there anything your partner shared that surprised you, or that you're still sitting with?

How confident do you feel about the rituals you agreed to? What might get in the way, and how will you handle that?

<table>
<tr><td>⏱ 20–25
minutes
total</td><td>Session time · can be split across two sittings if needed</td></tr>
</table>

The solo work in Chapter 7 goes to the roots of your physical language — where it came from, what it means to you, and what you most need that you may not have said clearly.

🌿 SOLO TRACK —Your Physical Language — Where It Came From

What forms of physical affection were present in the family you grew up in? Was touch common, rare, conditional, or absent?

How do you think what you grew up with shapes what you're comfortable giving and receiving now — in terms of touch, closeness, and physical presence?

What physical gesture from your partner makes you feel most loved and most connected? (Be specific — not "affection" but the actual gesture: a hand held in a specific way, a particular kind of hug, being reached for in the night.)

Have you told your partner this explicitly — in those specific terms? If not, why not? And: can you tell them this week?

Is there something about physical intimacy in this relationship that you've been wanting to say — or wanting to change — that you haven't said clearly? Write it here, using the Soft Startup format from Chapter 3 if it helps:
I feel _________________________ when _________________________ and what I'd love is _________________________.

Choose one physical gesture this week — something small, specific, and actionable by you alone. Not a conversation. A gesture.

Examples: the six-second kiss, introduced once today. A longer hug at homecoming. Reaching for your partner's hand during an evening in. Sitting close on the sofa when you'd usually sit separately. A hand on their shoulder as you pass.

Write the gesture you're committing to:

When, specifically, will you do it this week?

After you've done it, write what happened — even if what happened was subtle or small:

What did it feel like to initiate physical contact — to choose to close the distance, even slightly?

What This Week Is Really About

Chapter 7 is asking you to do something that can feel disproportionately vulnerable: to move toward your partner physically, even when the emotional distance between you hasn't fully closed yet.

For many people, initiating physical contact when things feel uncertain is one of the scariest things in this workbook. It requires you to risk something — rejection, or the awkwardness of a gesture that isn't immediately reciprocated, or the feeling of wanting something your partner may not be ready to give.

That risk is real. And it is also precisely where physical reconnection lives. You cannot rebuild physical closeness by waiting for your partner to initiate. You cannot rebuild it by waiting until everything else feels perfectly resolved. You rebuild it by beginning — by one small gesture, offered without guarantee of return, that says: I want to be closer to you.

The six-second kiss is not just a kiss. The longer hug is not just a hug. The hand reached for in the dark is not just a hand. Each of these gestures is a bid — in the language of Chapter 6 — for the specific form of connection that touch provides. And every bid accepted is a step back toward each other. perfectly resolved. You rebuild it by beginning — by one small gesture, offered without guarantee of return, that says: I want to be closer to you.

The six-second kiss is not just a kiss. The longer hug is not just a hug. The hand reached for in the dark is not just a hand. Each of these gestures is a bid — in the language of Chapter 6 — for the specific form of connection that touch provides. And every bid accepted is a step back toward each other.

Physical and emotional intimacy are not separate tracks. They inform each other continuously. The work you've done in Chapters 3 and 4 on communication, and the curiosity you started in Chapter 6, creates the ground on which physical reconnection grows. And the physical reconnection you start building this week creates the safety in which emotional openness deepens.
They feed each other. Start anywhere. Keep going.

☑ Week 7 Closing Ritual — 5 Minutes

□ Commit out loud to one specific physical ritual for this week — name it exactly (not "more affection" but the actual gesture, the actual moment)

□ Share one thing you learned about your partner's physical needs this week that surprised you or that you're glad you know

□ Do the six-second kiss — right now, if possible, or before the end of today

□ Appreciation: "The way you make me feel physically safe is..." — if this is hard to complete honestly, name that too

---

Optional — One Gesture, One Week

The physical ritual I'm committing to this week — specific and named:

The moment I plan to initiate it:

⚡ 10-Minute Version — When This Is All You Have

Two things, in ten minutes:

1. Complete the Physical Intimacy Check-In independently. Just the scores — you don't have to write the notes.

2. Share one score with your partner. Just one — the one that feels most important for them to know. Use the Attunement Ladder when they share theirs back.

Then do the six-second kiss. Tonight. That's the whole ten minutes.

You don't have to feel close before you reach for each other. Sometimes, you reach for each other in order to feel close. Begin with the gesture. Let the feeling follow.

Chapter 8

The Weight of Life

Navigating the Stressors That Pull Couples Apart

The most common relationship problems aren't relationship problems at all. They're life problems that land inside the relationship — and get mistaken for evidence that the relationship is broken.

⏱ 30 minutes total	*Session time · can be split across two sittings if needed*

🌿 SOLO TRACK — This chapter has its own exercises for the partner working alone. You'll find them in the Solo section below.

External Stressors, Internal Damage

There is a conversation that almost every couple eventually has — usually in the middle of a fight about something specific, something concrete, something that seems on the surface like a disagreement about money or the children or whose parents they're spending the holiday with — that ends with one or both of them wondering: is this about us, or is this about everything else?

The answer is almost always: both. And the failure to distinguish between the two is one of the most common sources of relational damage that isn't actually caused by the relationship.

External stressors — financial pressure, demanding careers, parenting disagreements, in-laws, illness, grief, the relentless logistics of running a shared life — do not stay neatly outside the relationship. They seep in.

They raise the baseline tension. They deplete the patience and goodwill that couples need to navigate ordinary friction well. They make small irritations feel like large patterns. They make a comment about the dishes feel like a comment about respect.

And critically: under stress, most people become worse versions of their communication selves. The Horsemen from Chapter 3 appear more readily. The ability to listen with attunement from Chapter 4 shrinks. The curiosity that Chapter 6 asks for becomes harder to access when the mind is occupied by worry or exhaustion.

None of this means the relationship is failing. It means the relationship is under load. Those are different things. A relationship under load needs different care than a relationship that is broken. This chapter is about understanding the load — and learning to carry it together rather than alone.

The argument started, as their arguments often did, with something specific: Jordan had missed a parent-teacher conference because of a client dinner he hadn't mentioned until the day before.

Maya heard: You don't prioritize this family.

Jordan heard: You can't do anything right.

They said versions of these things out loud. The argument lasted an hour and resolved nothing.

What neither of them said — what neither of them had found a way to say — was what was actually happening underneath. Jordan was three months into a performance review that might end his role. He hadn't told Maya because he didn't want her to worry, and because saying it out loud would make it more real. Maya was quietly terrified about money. Not because they were in crisis, but because she'd grown up in a family where financial instability had meant emotional instability, and any signal of financial uncertainty triggered something old and afraid in her.

They weren't fighting about the parent-teacher conference. They were fighting about fear — two different fears, both unspoken, both doing damage through the nearest available argument.

The relationship was not the problem. The relationship was where the problem was landing.

Facing Outward Together — The Team Reframe

Research on how external stress affects couples consistently finds one factor that determines whether stress damages a relationship or is weathered by it: whether the couple faces the stressor as a team or as two individuals who happen to share a home.

Couples who face external stress together — who say "us versus this problem" rather than "me versus you" — show dramatically higher resilience and relationship satisfaction, even when the stressor itself is severe. The act of naming a shared adversary, and consciously positioning yourselves on the same side of it, changes something fundamental about how the stress is experienced.

This is not primarily about problem-solving. Couples facing grief, illness, or financial pressures cannot always solve their way out. The team reframe is not about fixing the stressor — it's about not letting the stressor fix itself between you.

The most destructive thing external stress does to a relationship is not the stress itself. It's the way stressed people tend to treat the nearest available person as the source of their distress. The partner who is anxious about money criticizes the partner who forgot to pay a bill — not because the bill is the real issue, but because the bill is concrete and the fear is not. The parent who is overwhelmed by childcare snaps at the co-parent about something unrelated — because the overwhelm needs somewhere to go.

Noticing this pattern — catching yourself in the moment when you're about to use your partner as a container for stress that belongs somewhere else — is one of the most important skills in this chapter. It doesn't require you to manage your stress perfectly. It requires you to notice when you're misaddressing it.

Research by Neff and Karney (2009) found that the way couples handle external stress is a stronger predictor of relationship quality over time than the presence of the stress itself. Couples who used what the researchers called "capitalization" — sharing positive events together — and "stress-buffering" — facing difficulties as a unit — maintained relationship satisfaction even during high-stress periods, while couples who didn't showed significant deterioration.

Gottman's work on the "Stress-Reducing Conversation" identifies a specific format for discussing external stressors that prevents the conversation from becoming a conflict: each partner speaks about their experience of the stressor while the other listens without problem-solving, advising, or making it about themselves. The goal is not resolution — it is the felt experience of being accompanied in the difficulty.

Being understood in what you're carrying is not the same as having it removed. But it changes how heavy it feels.

Mapping What You're Currently Carrying

Before we move to specific stressor areas, it's worth taking stock of the full landscape of external pressure you're both navigating right now. This is not a complaint session. It is a recognition exercise — an acknowledgment, to yourself and your partner, of what is actually in the system.

Use the table below to map the external stressors currently present in your life. For each one that applies, note how it's showing up inside the relationship (not what's wrong with your partner — what you notice in yourself or in the dynamic between you), and one possible team-facing response.

Only fill in the stressors that are currently active. Leave blank rows as they are.

External stressor	How it's showing up inside the relationship	One team-facing response
Work / career pressure		
Financial tension		
Parenting demands		
Extended family / in-laws		
Health — yours or someone else's		
Grief or loss		
Other:		

Looking at your completed map: which stressor is most actively affecting how you show up in the relationship right now?

Is there a stressor you listed that your partner may not fully know about — or not know the depth of?

When this stressor shows up between you as an argument or tension, what form does it usually take?

Money — The Conversation Underneath the Argument

Financial conflict is one of the top three causes of relationship breakdown across almost every study that has examined it. And yet most couples never have a real conversation about their actual relationship with money. They have arguments about specific expenditures. They disagree about individual purchases, savings rates, priorities. They fight about whether a particular expense was justified.

These surface arguments are rarely about the specific expenditure. They are about something deeper: what money means to each person, what security looks like to them, what they believe they deserve, what they fear, and what they learned about money before they ever met their partner.
Two people who grew up with very different financial climates bring fundamentally different emotional architectures to money conversations.

Someone who grew up in a household where financial anxiety was constant may react to any unexpected expense with a fear response that seems disproportionate to the situation — because for them, unexpected expenses are encoded as danger, not inconvenience. Someone who grew up in abundance may spend freely in ways that feel irresponsible to their partner — not because they don't care about security, but because they have a different felt sense of what security is.

These are not character flaws. They are origins. And understanding your partner's origin story around money — and sharing your own — changes the texture of every financial conversation you will have.

📖 Maya and Jordan — What Money Means

Maya's family had been comfortable until she was eleven, when her father's business failed. She remembered very specifically the night her parents told her they were moving. The conversation in the kitchen. The way her mother's voice was carefully controlled. The sense that the world had been revealed as more precarious than she'd understood.

She had carried that knowledge forward. She had an emergency fund that made Jordan smile, gently. She tracked every expense. She was, he sometimes said — affectionately, she assumed — a little intense about money.

Jordan had grown up without that scare. His parents were not wealthy, but they were steady. Money had been present enough that it never felt like a threat. He spent freely within what he considered reasonable limits. He was not irresponsible. He simply did not feel the urgency that Maya felt.

"You worry too much," he had said once, early in their relationship.
What Maya heard: your fear is irrational. What she felt: my fear is invisible to you.

They had never sat down and told each other these stories. They had just kept colliding at the intersection of them.

Financial conflict almost always looks like an argument about money. It is almost always an argument about safety.

Money Origin Story — For Each Partner

Growing up, what was the emotional climate around money in your family? (Anxious? Abundant? Secretive? Chaotic? Steady?)

What belief about money have you carried into this relationship — something you've rarely examined or named out loud?

When you and your partner disagree about money, what are you usually really afraid of underneath the specific disagreement?

One financial conversation we've been avoiding that we need to have:

For couples with children, parenting disagreements carry a particular charge. The stakes feel enormous. Each partner is operating from a deeply held sense of what children need, what parenting should look like, and what the consequences of getting it wrong might be — and those senses are often in tension.

Each partner carries a parenting template from their own childhood: the way they were raised, what worked, what didn't, what they swore they would do differently and what they unconsciously replicated. These templates are rarely made explicit. They operate in the background — informing reactions to discipline decisions, screen time limits, emotional responses to children's distress — until they collide with a partner's different template.

The key insight that changes parenting conflict: you are allowed to parent differently from each other in style, tone, and specific approach while agreeing on the values underneath. Two parents can have different thresholds for mess, different comfort levels with risk-taking, different ideas about how much autonomy a seven-year-old should have — and still be fundamentally aligned on what matters most. The alignment on core values (safety, respect, emotional honesty, resilience) is more important, and more achievable, than agreement on every decision.

Parenting conflict also has a secondary layer that is worth naming: it is often a vehicle for couples to have the argument they haven't been able to have directly. A disagreement about how to handle a child's tantrum is sometimes really a disagreement about whose emotional needs are being heard. A fight about screen time can carry the weight of a broader argument about priorities and who in the family has the authority to decide them.

The Money Origin Story exercise in the previous section has a direct parallel here.
Your parenting approach is not arbitrary — it has roots. Understanding where your
partner's approach comes from is as important as agreeing on where it should go.

List your three most important values for how you want to raise your children — the
things you most want them to experience, learn, or feel:

1. ____

2. ____

3. ____

Where do you feel most aligned with your partner as a parenting team? What do you
do well together?

Where do you feel most in conflict — and what do you think is usually underneath
that conflict for you? (Not what's wrong with your partner's approach, but what fear
or value of yours is being activated.)

Where do you think your parenting approach comes from — what in your own
childhood is it shaped by?

One thing I most need from my partner as a co-parent that I haven't asked for clearly:

If you don't have children, the parenting section doesn't apply directly — but the underlying principle does. Every partnership has an equivalent: an area where each partner has a strong, deeply-held sense of how things should be done, shaped by their history, that collides with their partner's equally strong sense.

It might be how you manage the home. How you handle illness. How you relate to extended family. How you approach social obligations. Whatever area that has the texture of parenting conflict in your relationship — high stakes, strong feelings, frequent collision — apply this section's questions there instead.

Other External Pressures — Naming What Else Is in the Room

Money and parenting are two of the most universal stressors couples navigate, but they are not the only ones. Careers that demand too much, in-laws whose involvement creates friction, friendships that have shifted, health concerns — yours, a child's, a parent's — grief, illness, political stress, housing pressure, the relentless administration of modern life.
Each of these has its own particular way of entering a relationship.

Career pressure tends to produce scarcity of time and presence — one or both partners are chronically elsewhere. Extended family friction tends to produce loyalty conflicts and the exhausting performance of family harmony. Grief produces a particular isolation — each partner grieving differently, sometimes unable to reach across to each other in the loss.

Health concerns introduce fear into the relationship's daily texture, fear that often cannot be spoken about directly and so travels sideways.
The exercise that matters most across all of these is not the one in this chapter.

It is the one you do in the Stress-Reducing Conversation in the Together Track below: taking turns speaking honestly about one external stressor while your partner listens without fixing, without problem-solving, without making it about themselves. Being accompanied in the weight of something is often the most relief available.

There is a version of this that the solo reader can do, and it is in the Solo Track. It is not the same as being accompanied — but it is not nothing, either. Naming what you're carrying, even to yourself, clarifies what the load actually is and makes it less likely to be misdirected.

When you find yourself in an argument with your partner that feels disproportionate to its stated subject — when the emotion in the room is larger than the specific issue would explain — try asking yourself:

"Is this actually about us? Or is this something from outside the relationship that has found its way in?"

You do not have to answer this question out loud, in the middle of the argument. But you can carry it as a quiet reference point. If the answer is "something from outside has found its way in," the conversation that's needed is not a debate about the presenting issue. It's the one where you say: "I think I've been carrying something that's not really about you. Can I tell you what it is?"

That sentence — offered genuinely — changes the entire architecture of what comes next.

Together Track — Session 8

⏱ 25 minutes total	*Session time · can be split across two sittings if needed*

This session uses a specific format developed from Gottman's research on stress-reducing conversation. It has a clear structure, and the structure matters. Follow it closely — especially the listener's constraints, which are tighter than in any other session in this workbook.

The Stress-Reducing Conversation — Format

Choose one external stressor that is currently creating tension in or around your relationship. It should be something outside the relationship itself — work, finances, family, health, logistics — not a grievance about your partner.

Each partner gets five minutes to speak about their experience of this stressor. During those five minutes, use the Attunement Ladder from Chapter 4 as your listener framework. Specifically:

 offer advice, solutions, or reassurance. May not say "it'll be fine" or "here's what you should do." May not redirect to their own experience. May not defend themselves if the stressor is one that involves them.

 notice, reflect, validate, and empathize. Ask clarifying questions only to understand better, not to redirect. Hold the speaker's experience without trying to change it.

After both partners have spoken: together, identify one concrete thing you can do this week as a team to face this stressor — even something small. The act of taking one aligned action creates the felt sense of being on the same side.

Close the session with a genuine acknowledgment to each other:
"I see how hard you're working with [this stressor]. That matters to me."

After the Stress-Reducing Conversation

What was it like to speak about your stressor without your partner jumping to solutions?

What was it like to listen without problem-solving — to simply be present with your partner's experience of the difficulty?

The one team action we agreed to take this week:

The acknowledgment I want to give my partner — what I see them carrying, named specifically:

<table>
<tr><td>⏱ 20–25 minutes total</td><td>Session time · can be split across two sittings if needed</td></tr>
</table>

The solo work in Chapter 8 asks you to do something that can be surprisingly difficult: to be honest with yourself about what you're carrying — and then to consider what it would mean to stop carrying it alone.

🌿 SOLO TRACK — What Are You Carrying?
Complete the Stressor Map above on your own. Then take your time with these questions.

What external stressor is currently affecting your relationship the most — that you haven't directly talked about with your partner?

How is this stressor showing up in how you treat your partner — even when the argument or tension seems to be about something else?

Why haven't you talked about it directly? What stops you — fear of burdening them, fear of their reaction, a belief that you should be able to handle it yourself, something else?

What would it look like to invite your partner into this stressor — not to solve it, but simply to know about it? What would you need to say?

Think of a recent argument or moment of tension with your partner that felt disproportionate to what it was ostensibly about.

What was the stated subject of the tension?

What external stressor was present in your life at the time?

Looking back: what percentage of the tension was really about your partner's behavior, and what percentage was the external stressor finding a target?

If you could go back to that moment with what you know now, what would you say instead — using the Soft Startup from Chapter 3 to name what was actually going on for you?

I feel ____ because

____ and what I actually

need is ____.

Is there a moment this week when you could say something like this to your partner — naming the real source of the tension rather than the presenting one?

Chapter 8 sits at the end of Part Three — the Connection section — and it completes something that Chapters 6 and 7 began. Connection is not only built in the warm moments, in the love map questions and the six-second kisses. It is also built in the hard moments — in the willingness to face the difficult things together rather than alone.

The couples who stay close over decades are not the ones who avoid external stress. Stress is not avoidable. They are the ones who have learned — through practice, not through natural gift — to face the things that arrive from outside the relationship without turning those things on each other.

This is the chapter's core ask: to distinguish between "something hard is happening" and "my partner is the problem." These can feel identical when you're flooded and exhausted. They are not the same. And the willingness to make that distinction — even imperfectly, even belatedly, even by saying "I think I've been taking something out on you that isn't really about you" — is one of the most generous things you can offer a partner.

The Stress-Reducing Conversation is a tool you can return to repeatedly. It doesn't expire after this week. Every time something external is creating pressure between you — every time you notice that arguments are more frequent or more charged than usual — this is the format to reach for. Name the stressor. Face it outward. Take one small action together.
Life will keep bringing weight. The question is whether you carry it separately or together. Together is always lighter.

□ Name one external stressor you faced this week — together or separately
□ Identify one moment, however brief, when you felt like you were on the same team
□ Appreciation: "Something I appreciate about how you carry the weight of our life is..." — be specific
□ Set your session time for Week 9 — you are entering Part Four, the final section

Describe one moment this week — however small — when you and your partner faced something together rather than separately:

What made it feel like you were on the same side in that moment?

One thing, done well, in ten minutes:

Choose one external stressor. Each partner takes two minutes to describe how it's affecting them — not what should be done about it, not whose fault it is, just how it feels. The listener uses Rungs 1–3 of the Attunement Ladder: notice, reflect, validate.

Then agree on one tiny team action — something concrete and achievable this week. Shake on it.

The relief of being accompanied in difficulty does not require a long conversation. It requires a real one.

A thought to carry into Part Four:
You have spent eight weeks learning to communicate more honestly, listen more generously, connect more deliberately, and face the difficult things without losing each other in them. Part Four asks a final question: what are you building this for?

Chapter 9

The Future We're Building

Creating Shared Meaning, Rituals, and a Life Worth Choosing Every Day

The couples who thrive aren't the ones without problems. They're the ones who have built something together that feels worth protecting.

○30 minutes total	Session time · can be split across two sittings if needed

SOLO TRACK — This chapter has its own exercises for the partner working alone. You'll find them in the Solo section below.

From Surviving to Creating

Something shifts when you reach Week 9.

The first eight chapters of this workbook were largely about repair — about finding the honest coordinates of your relationship (Chapter 1), examining the stories you've been telling yourselves (Chapter 2), learning to speak and listen with more skill and less damage (Chapters 3 and 4), facing conflict and external pressure without losing each other in it (Chapters 5 and 8), and rebuilding the emotional and physical closeness that had quietly eroded (Chapters 6 and 7).

All of that work was necessary. And all of it was, in a sense, remedial — moving the relationship from where it was to something more solid, more honest, more navigable.

Part Four asks a different question. Not: how do we fix what's broken? But: what do we want to build?

This is the shift that Gottman describes in what he calls the top level of the Sound Relationship House: Creating Shared Meaning. It is the level at which a partnership transforms from a functional arrangement — two people managing a shared life — into something intentional. A relationship with its own culture, its own symbols, its own rituals that say this is us. A relationship built toward something, not just maintained against entropy.

The couples who thrive over decades are not the ones who have solved every problem. They are the ones who have built something together that feels worth coming back to — worth protecting, worth choosing again on the ordinary Tuesday when nothing is particularly romantic or dramatic, and staying is simply the right thing to do.

This chapter is about building that thing deliberately. Not waiting for it to emerge. Building it.

📖 Maya and Jordan — The Thursday Night Question

It was a Thursday evening. Phoebe was in bed. They'd had the six-second kiss at the front door — a habit that still felt slightly formal to both of them but that both of them had noticed, quietly, was doing something. They were sitting at the kitchen table with the workbook between them.

"I've been thinking about Thursday nights," Maya said.

Jordan looked up.

"We used to have pasta. Before everything. I want to go back to that. Not the pasta specifically — I want to go back to the feeling that Thursday was ours."

Jordan was quiet for a moment. Then: "I didn't know you missed that."
"I didn't know I did either," she said. "Not until I started writing things down."

That week they made pasta. It was nothing special — a weeknight, Phoebe's toys still on the living room floor, the kitchen not entirely tidy.

But something in it felt like a choice. Like they had decided, consciously, what kind of couple they wanted to be.

That decision — small, specific, unheroic — is what shared meaning is made of.

The Three Pillars of Shared Meaning

Research on long-term relationship satisfaction consistently identifies three components that distinguish couples who build lasting, thriving partnerships from those who merely maintain functional ones. Gottman calls these collectively the architecture of shared meaning.

Read each pillar carefully. Then notice which one feels most present in your relationship right now — and which one feels most absent.

Rituals of Connection	Shared Values & Legacy	Individual Dreams Held Together
Regular, repeated activities both partners associate with warmth and identity as a couple. Not just date night — the specific, idiosyncratic traditions that say: this is us.	Conscious agreement about what you stand for as a couple — what you want to transmit, how you want to live, what you want your relationship to mean beyond the two of you.	Each partner has personal aspirations that belong to them alone. A great partnership doesn't absorb those dreams — it holds them, supports them, makes room for them.

What the Research Shows

Gottman's longitudinal research found that couples who actively cultivate shared meaning — through rituals, shared values, and mutual support for individual dreams — show significantly higher relationship satisfaction, resilience during conflict, and long-term stability. The 'Sound Relationship House' model positions shared meaning as the apex: the level that everything below it supports, and without which the structure lacks a purpose.

Interestingly, shared meaning doesn't require agreement on everything. Couples with quite different individual interests, careers, and even values can build strong shared meaning — as long as they are conscious and deliberate about the specific areas they are building together. The shared meaning doesn't have to be total. It has to be real.

What makes a ritual a ritual — rather than just a habit — is that both partners know it matters and choose to protect it. The intentionality is the ingredient.

Rituals of Connection — The Specific, the Small, the Yours

"Date night" is not a ritual. A ritual is something more particular: a specific, repeated activity that both partners have implicitly or explicitly agreed belongs to them as a couple. Something that, when it happens, produces a quiet recognition — this is us.

For some couples it's Sunday morning coffee before anyone else wakes up.

For others it's a particular walk they've taken for years, or a shared television ritual, or the way they make dinner together on Friday evenings, or a private vocabulary of jokes that would be incomprehensible to anyone else. For Maya and Jordan it was Thursday night pasta — not because pasta is meaningful, but because the choice to make time for each other in the middle of an ordinary week was.

Rituals of connection serve several functions simultaneously. They create predictable islands of togetherness in weeks that are otherwise dominated by logistics. They build what researchers call "positive sentiment reserve" — the accumulated goodwill that protects a relationship during difficult periods. And they create identity: a sense of us as a particular kind of couple, with particular things that belong to us.

When rituals disappear — as they often do under the pressure of children, demanding careers, and the general administration of life — they take some of that identity with them. One of the simplest and most effective things a couple can do in Part Four of this workbook is to name the rituals they have, protect the ones worth keeping, and consciously create new ones.

The most durable rituals are also the most ordinary. Grand romantic gestures are memorable but not repeatable. A Thursday night that is reliably, unremarkably yours is something you can actually build a relationship on.

Shared Values and Legacy — What You Stand For Together

Most couples have never explicitly discussed what they stand for. They have individual values — things they believe privately, principles they apply in their own lives — but the question of what their partnership stands for, as a unit, goes largely unexamined.

This is not because it doesn't matter. It matters enormously. A couple that has never named its shared values is like an organization that has never written its mission: everyone is working, but not necessarily toward the same thing, and there is no shared language for resolving the moments when different priorities collide.

Shared values are not the same as identical beliefs. Two people can hold the same value — honesty, say, or generosity — and express it in quite different ways, with different emphases, in different domains of life. What shared values provide is not uniformity but a common frame: a set of commitments that both partners agree are worth working toward, even when the work is inconvenient.

The question of legacy — what you want your relationship to mean, beyond the two of you, and what you want to transmit to those who know you — is related but distinct. Legacy thinking is not available to every couple; it requires a certain stability and groundedness that not all relationships have reached by Week 9. But for couples who are ready for it, the legacy question is clarifying in ways that few others are. It asks: if your relationship were described honestly, years from now, what would you want said? And more usefully: what are you doing today that moves toward that description?

Individual Dreams Held Together

The third pillar is the one most couples find hardest to talk about — not because it's painful, but because it requires each partner to admit to wanting something that belongs only to them.

Intimate relationships carry a quiet pressure toward convergence. The longer two people are together, the more their lives merge — practically, socially, economically. This merging is largely a good thing. But it can carry a cost: the gradual suppression of individual desires, ambitions, and dreams that don't fit neatly into the shared life. Jordan's franchise research — eighteen months of quiet investigation that he'd never mentioned because he assumed Maya would find it impractical — is one version of this. A partner who has quietly stopped pursuing a creative project. A partner who has set aside a professional aspiration because the timing never seems right. A partner who has a clear picture of something they want for their own life that they've never asked the other person to help hold.

Gottman's research identifies what he calls "dreams within conflict" — the personal dreams and aspirations that are embedded in even the most entrenched relationship arguments. The couple who fights about money is often fighting, underneath, about whose vision of the future will prevail. The couple who fights about time allocation is often fighting about whose individual needs are being seen.

A partnership that is large enough to hold both partners' individual dreams — not by absorbing them, but by actively making room for them — is not only more satisfying for both people. It is also more stable. Partners who feel that their personal aspirations are supported within the relationship don't need to carry those aspirations as secret grievances or unexploded tensions. They can bring them into the open, where they can be discussed, planned for, and — when possible — actively built toward.

When your partner shares a personal dream — whether in this chapter's exercise or in an ordinary conversation — the response that matters most is not assessment of feasibility. It is understanding of meaning.

Before asking "how would that work?" or "is that realistic?", ask: "Tell me more about what that dream means to you." And then listen — the way you practiced in Chapter 4 — with the Attunement Ladder rather than with an evaluating mind.

Your partner's dream does not have to be convenient for you to be valid. Supporting a dream doesn't require you to sacrifice your own. It requires you to be genuinely curious about what your partner wants from their life, and to say — explicitly, out loud — that you want them to have it.

That kind of witness — being truly seen in what you want — is one of the deepest forms of intimacy available in a long partnership.

Building Your Shared Meaning Map

Complete the exercise below independently before comparing with your partner. Your lists don't have to match — in fact, the differences are often more interesting than the similarities, and they create the most useful conversations.

BUILDING OUR SHARED MEANING MAP

Complete independently. Your lists don't have to match — the differences are worth discussing.

Rituals & traditions already part of our relationship (however small — even a Sunday morning coffee routine counts):

Rituals or traditions I'd like to create, reclaim, or protect:

Values I most want our relationship to actively embody — things I'm willing to work toward, not just aspire to:

One personal dream I have — that I'd love my partner to know about and actively support:

Which ritual or tradition that your partner listed surprised you — or that you hadn't thought of yourself?

Where are your values lists most aligned? Where are they most different — and what does that difference tell you?

Your partner shared a personal dream. What is your first response to hearing it — and what do you want them to know about how you hold that dream?

One of the most clarifying exercises in long-term relationship work is writing a joint vision statement: a brief, honest description of the relationship you are intentionally building. Not what you have now. Not what you hope to have someday, vaguely. What you are actively working toward.

A vision statement is not a fantasy. It is not a list of things you want your partner to change. It is a shared declaration of intention — the two of you naming, together, what kind of partnership you are building and what you are willing to do to build it.

The prompts below are a scaffold. Use them as a starting point, then write in your own words. The final version should sound like you — like the specific, particular two of you — rather than like something from a greeting card.

Some couples post their finished vision statement somewhere visible. Some keep it in the workbook and return to it periodically. Some write it and find that the act of writing it together was the exercise, and don't need to display it anywhere. All of these are right.

> **OUR RELATIONSHIP VISION STATEMENT — Draft Together**
> *Complete the prompts below together, each contributing words and ideas. This doesn't have to be polished. It has to be honest.*
> *We are building a relationship that is...*
>
>
> *We protect it by...*
>
>
> *We are at our best together when...*
>
>
> *What we most want our relationship to feel like is...*

Final version — write it here once you've settled on the words you both mean:

Optional: write or print this somewhere you'll both see it — on a phone lock screen, a kitchen wall, the inside of a journal.

Together Track — Session 9

⏱ **20 minutes total** | *Session time · can be split across two sittings if needed*

This session has two parts. The first is drafting your Relationship Vision Statement together — using the prompts above and anything else that feels true. The second is each partner sharing one personal dream and being witnessed in it.

Part 1 — Draft the Vision Statement (15 minutes)

Work through the vision statement prompts together. Don't aim for perfection on the first pass — say what you actually mean, even if it comes out awkwardly. The best vision statements are slightly messy and feel true rather than polished and feel aspirational.

If you find yourselves stuck, use the Shared Meaning Map entries as raw material: what rituals do you both want to protect? What values keep appearing in both your lists? What does the relationship feel like at its best? That feeling is the vision — your task is to find words for it.

Part 2 — The Dream Conversation (10 minutes)

Each partner shares one personal dream — something they want for themselves, from their own life, that they'd love their partner to know about and support. This is not a request. It is a disclosure.

The listener's role is explicit and constrained: do not evaluate feasibility. Do not offer solutions or timelines. Do not make the dream about yourself. Your only task is to understand what this dream means to your partner — and to say, genuinely, that you want them to have it.

The Dream Conversation — Listener's Only Job

When your partner shares their dream, respond with curiosity first:

"Tell me more about what that dream means to you."

"When did you start wanting that?"

"What would it feel like to be moving toward it?"

After listening: tell your partner one true thing about how you feel, hearing them share this. Not a plan. Not a condition. Just: what it means to you to know this about them.

After the Session — What We Built

How did it feel to write the vision statement together — even the imperfect draft version?

What is the dream your partner shared? Write it here so you remember it clearly:

What do you want your partner to know about how you hold that dream for them?

Solo Track — For the Partner Working Alone

⏱ 20–25 minutes total — *Session time · can be split across two sittings if needed*

The solo work in Chapter 9 asks you to hold the vision for the relationship yourself — knowing that your partner may not be there yet, and that your holding it is still worthwhile. Some of the most powerful relationship work happens when one person decides what they want to build and begins building toward it, alone if necessary, trusting that the direction matters even without confirmation.

If your relationship is exactly as you hope it will be in three years — not perfect, but moving in the right direction — what does it look and feel like? Describe it concretely: what does a typical Tuesday look like? What is the atmosphere between you?

Of the three pillars — Rituals of Connection, Shared Values, and Individual Dreams Held Together — which one feels most missing from your relationship right now?

What is one ritual you could introduce or reclaim — this week, unilaterally, without requiring your partner's formal agreement — that would begin to move toward the relationship you described above?

What is one personal dream of yours that your partner doesn't fully know about? What stops you from telling them?

Write a solo version of the vision statement — not what both of you are building (you can't write that alone), but what you are building toward, personally, in how you show up in this relationship:
The partner I am working to become is...

The relationship I am working to help build is...

One thing I will keep choosing, even when it's hard, is...

Choose one action you can take this week — without waiting for your partner — that moves toward the relationship you described above. It should be something small and concrete.

The action:

Why this one:

After you've done it, note what happened — even if what happened was subtle:

What This Week Is Really About

Chapter 9 is the pivot point of the book. Every chapter before it was about understanding, repairing, and reconnecting. This chapter asks something new: to look forward.

Looking forward — deciding what you want to build, naming it, committing to it even in draft form — is harder than it might appear. It requires you to believe that the future is something you have agency over. That the relationship you have is not simply the relationship you ended up with, but one you are continuously choosing and shaping.
For couples who have been in distress for a long time, this belief is not always easy to access. The weight of accumulated hurt, unmet needs, and hardened patterns can make the future feel predetermined rather than open. Part of what the previous eight weeks have been doing — gradually, through practice — is loosening that sense of predetermination. Showing, in small but real ways, that things can be different.

The vision statement you wrote this week is not a contract. It is not a verdict on how things currently are. It is a direction — a compass bearing for the choices you will make in the coming weeks and months when the workbook is on the shelf and ordinary life resumes.

Ordinary life is where relationships are actually built. Not in the sessions, not in the exercises, but in the ordinary evening when you could reach for your partner or your phone, and you choose your partner. In the moment when the argument starts to escalate and you remember the Soft Startup. In the Thursday when you make pasta not because you planned it but because you both decided, at some point in the preceding weeks, that Thursday was worth protecting.

That is the vision becoming real. Not all at once. One Thursday at a time.

☑ **Week 9 Closing Ritual — 5 Minutes**
□ Share one moment from this week that felt like the relationship you're building toward — however small
□ Name one ritual you want to protect, create, or reclaim — and say it specifically
□ Appreciation: "Something about the future I'm looking forward to with you is..." — let yourself mean it
□ Set your session time for Week 10 — the final chapter

◁▭ **Optional — Our Vision, in Our Words**
Write the line from your vision statement that feels most true — the one you want to carry into this week:

⚡ **10-Minute Version — When This Is All You Have**
Three things, in ten minutes:
1. Each partner names one ritual they want to protect or create.
2. Each partner shares one personal dream — no evaluation, just disclosure.
3. Together, complete one sentence: "We are building a relationship that is..."
One sentence. Agreed on, together. That is enough for today.

A thought to carry into Week 10:
You have named what you're building. The final chapter asks how you keep building it — after the workbook closes, after the sessions end, in the ordinary weeks when no one is asking you to show up and you show up anyway.

Chapter 10

The Relationship You Keep Choosing

Trust, Repair and the Habits That Make Love Last

You don't build a great relationship once. You build it again, every day, in a thousand small choices most people never notice they're making.

⏱ 35 minutes total	*Session time · can be split across two sittings if needed*

🌿 SOLO TRACK — This chapter has its own exercises for the partner working alone. You'll find them in the Solo section below.

Trust as Architecture

You have reached the last chapter. Before anything else, that is worth naming.

Ten weeks ago you opened this book somewhere — perhaps alone, on your side of the bed, at 11pm after an argument that went nowhere. Perhaps with your partner, tentative and slightly skeptical, not sure what you were agreeing to. Perhaps in the middle of something that felt very close to the end of the road.

You are not in the same place now. The relationship is not the same. Something has shifted — in how you see your partner, in how you speak to them, in what you understand about what the difficulty between you has actually been about. The shift may be small. It may be larger than you expected. Either way, it is real.

Chapter 10 is about what happens next. Not in the next ten weeks — in the next ten years. In the ordinary, unstructured, workbook-free life that resumes on the other side of this session.

The central concept of this chapter is one that runs beneath everything this workbook has asked of you: trust. Not trust as a binary — something you have or don't have — but trust as Gottman describes it: a sliding window, built in small deposits and eroded in small withdrawals, constructed not in grand moments but in the accumulated pattern of ordinary ones.

The good news embedded in this understanding: because trust is built in small moments, it can be rebuilt in small moments. You don't need a grand gesture. You need a hundred small ones, reliably delivered. You have been practicing that for ten weeks. This chapter asks you to keep practicing — after the structure falls away.

📖 Maya and Jordan — A Year Later

It was a Thursday evening, a year after Maya had put the workbook on the kitchen table.

Phoebe was in bed. Jordan had texted at 6 to say he'd be home by 7. He was. Maya had made pasta — not because it was a rule, but because they'd decided, at some point in the preceding year, that Thursday was worth protecting.

They didn't talk about anything important. They talked about Phoebe's teacher, about a documentary Jordan wanted to watch, about whether the kitchen needed repainting. They held hands for a few minutes after dinner, watching the rain on the window.

It was not a dramatic evening. It was not a romantic evening, in any way that a film would recognize. It was two people, sitting in their shared life, choosing each other in the small and unremarkable and entirely sufficient way that sustains a relationship across years.

The workbook was on the shelf. They had returned to it twice — once after a rough patch six months in, once when Jordan finally told Maya about the franchise idea and they spent three weeks deciding, together, that it was worth pursuing. The book had been a tool. They had become something more than the people who needed it.

Not fixed. Not finished. Just: still going. Still choosing. Still learning. Together.

The ATTUNE Framework — Trust in Daily Practice

Gottman's ATTUNE model distills the trust-building practice of a healthy long-term relationship into six elements. Each one corresponds to something this workbook has asked you to practice over the past ten weeks. Together, they form a daily framework — not a once-a-week exercise but a continuous orientation toward your partner.

Read through the framework carefully. Then use the self-assessment table that follows to score yourself honestly on each element and identify one specific way to practice it this week.

A	Awareness	Notice your partner's emotional state — not just their words. Catch the shift in tone, the quietness, the edge in their voice before it becomes a confrontation.
T	Turning Toward	Respond to bids for connection, especially the small ones. The comment that gets a reply. The hand that finds a hand back. The look acknowledged rather than missed.
T	Tolerance	Accept your partner's imperfections without contempt. Not suppress — accept. The person you chose comes with their whole self, including the parts that require patience.
U	Understanding	Genuinely try to understand your partner's perspective before asserting your own. Understanding is not agreement. It is prior to agreement, and often more important.
N	Non-Defensive Listening	Receive concern and feedback without deflecting. Let what your partner says about their experience actually land, rather than immediately building the case for your innocence.
E	Empathy	Feel with them, not just about them. The difference is presence: not observing your partner's distress from outside it, but allowing yourself to be moved by it.

Score yourself 1–5 on each element (1 = rarely, 5 = consistently). Be honest, not kind to yourself — this is a tool for growth, not a report card.

Element	Score 1–5	One specific way to practice this week
A — Awareness	___	
T — Turning Toward	___	
T — Tolerance	___	
U — Understanding	___	
N — Non-Defensive Listening	___	
E — Empathy	___	

Which element scored lowest — and what do you think gets in the way of that one specifically?

Which element has improved the most over the past ten weeks?

If your partner completed this assessment about you, what do you think they'd score differently from your own ratings — and why?

Repair — The Most Underrated Skill in This Book

There is a skill this workbook has touched on in passing — in Chapter 5's conflict section — that deserves a fuller treatment here, in the final chapter, because it may be the most important thing you take forward.
Repair.

Repair is what happens after things go wrong. And things will go wrong. The Horsemen will appear. The hard startup will happen before you remember the soft one. An external stressor will find its way in as an argument about something unrelated. A bid for connection will be missed, and the partner who made it will feel the familiar loneliness of not being received.

This is not failure. This is what being in a relationship with another person actually looks like, even after ten weeks of structured work, even for couples who are genuinely committed to each other.

What distinguishes the couples who thrive over time is not the absence of rupture. It is the speed and quality of repair. Gottman's research shows that repair attempts — any word, gesture, or action that tries to de-escalate conflict and reconnect — are among the single most powerful predictors of long-term relationship success.

Crucially, it's not even the quality of the repair attempt that matters most. It's whether the partner receives it.

The agreement to repair — the mutual understanding that when things go sideways, you come back, you say sorry, you reconnect, before resentment has time to harden — is one of the most important agreements two people can make about a relationship.

What Repair Actually Looks Like

Repair does not require a formal conversation. It does not require waiting until the perfect moment. It does not require either partner to be entirely in the wrong. Repair looks like:

A touch on the arm after a tense exchange, before either person has said anything.

"I'm sorry I said that the way I said it." Not: "I'm sorry you felt hurt." A real apology for a real thing.

"Can we try that again?" An invitation to restart. Offered gently, without accusation.

"I think I was taking something out on you." The acknowledgment from Chapter 8's diagnostic question, delivered.

A text the next morning that says: "Yesterday was hard. I love you." No more required.

The repair signal in your Maintenance Plan — the one you're agreeing to this week — is your shortcut to this. An agreed code between two people that means: I know this went wrong and I'm choosing you anyway.

What Happens After This Book

The ten weeks of structured work in this book are a beginning. A significant beginning — but a beginning. The skills you have practiced require maintenance. The insights you have reached require revisiting. The relationship you have been building requires continued choosing.

The most successful couples who complete structured programs like this one share three habits going forward. They are not complicated. They are not time-consuming. They require only intention and consistency.

The Weekly Check-In

Fifteen minutes, once a week, in the same place, at the same time. Not a problem-solving session. Not a conflict forum. A temperature check: how are we each really doing? What do I appreciate about you this week? Is there anything I need you to know? What are we looking forward to?

The weekly check-in is how you stay ahead of drift. It is how you catch the small misalignments before they calcify into patterns. It is the fifteen minutes that costs almost nothing and protects everything that costs everything to rebuild.

The Repair Commitment

The explicit agreement that when things go wrong — and they will — you come back. You do not let a rupture harden into silence for days. You do not add the unrepaired argument to the ledger of unspoken grievances. You find the moment, sooner rather than later, and you say: I know that didn't go well. I'm still choosing you.

This commitment does not require either person to be faultless. It requires both people to value the relationship above their need to be right.

The Return Clause

An explicit agreement about when you will return to this book or seek outside support — framed not as crisis intervention but as maintenance. Name the specific warning signs you will watch for. Not "if things get bad again" but the actual early signals you both know: the weeks when the Horsemen return consistently, when the weekly check-in stops happening, when the distance between you in the bed starts to grow again. Returning to structured support is not failure. It is the same reason you service a car: not because something has broken, but because maintenance is what keeps things from breaking.

> ### What the Research Shows
>
> Research on couples who complete structured therapeutic programs consistently finds that the presence of a maintenance plan — even a simple one — significantly predicts long-term gains. Couples who articulate specific agreements about how they will sustain new behaviors show substantially better outcomes at six-month and twelve-month follow-up than those who complete the program without one.
>
> The mechanism is not complicated: the maintenance plan creates accountability, provides a shared language for recognizing drift, and reduces the shame barrier to returning when things get difficult. Couples with a plan know what "difficult enough to act" looks like, rather than waiting until things are severe.
>
> *The Maintenance Plan you fill in today is not a contract with perfection. It is an agreement about what you will do when perfection fails — which is the only agreement that actually matters.*

✏ THE RELATIONSHIP MAINTENANCE PLAN — Our Agreements Going Forward

Fill this in together. Sign it if that makes it feel real. Keep it somewhere you'll both see it.

Our weekly check-in ritual:

When: ___________________________ Where: ___________________________ How long: _____________

What we'll cover each week (circle or add your own):
How we each really are · One appreciation · One thing that needs attention · Something we're looking forward to:

When things escalate, our agreed repair signal is:

We will return to this workbook — or seek outside support — if we notice:
(Name specific early warning signs — not "if things get bad" but the actual signals you both recognize)

The three habits from this workbook we most want to maintain:

1. ____

2. ____

3. ____

Our commitment to each other, going forward — in our own words:

Signed: ___________________________________ ___________________________________ Date: _____________

<table>
<tr><td>○ 35
minutes
total</td><td>The final session - take your time</td></tr>
</table>

This session has two parts. The first is completing and signing the Relationship Maintenance Plan above — making it a real, named agreement between two people. The second is the most important conversation in this workbook: looking back at what you've built, and looking forward at what you intend to keep building

There is no framework for this conversation beyond the one you've already learned. Listen the way Chapter 4 taught you. Speak the way Chapter 3 asked you to. Be curious the way Chapter 6 practiced. Be honest. Be present. Let this person sitting across from you matter to you — today, in this room, for these thirty-five minutes — the way they have always mattered, underneath all the difficulty..

☑ FINAL SESSION — Take Turns Sharing Your Answers
Each partner answers all five questions. The listener follows the same principle as every session in this workbook: receive first, respond second. There are no wrong answers. There is only honesty.
1. What was the most important thing you learned about yourself in this process?

2. What was the most important thing you learned about your partner?

3. What moment in the last ten weeks felt most like the relationship you want to have?

4. What do you want to remember to do when things get hard again?

5. What are you most grateful for about this person sitting across from you right now?

The most important thing my partner said in the final session that I want to hold onto:

The moment in the past ten weeks I most want to remember — and why:

Solo Track — For the Partner Working Alone

A Note for the Solo Reader on the Last Chapter

If you've worked through this book alone, the fact that you're still here — at the final chapter, ten weeks in — is itself a profound act of love. For your partner, and for yourself.

The work you've done is real. The changes you've made in how you communicate, how you listen, how you show up in difficult moments — your partner has almost certainly noticed, even if they haven't named it. Individual change within a relationship always creates relational change. The research on this is consistent. You have moved something.
Whatever happens next in your relationship, you know something now that you didn't know ten weeks ago: you are capable of this. You can hold a relationship with both hands and choose it, even when it's hard, even when it isn't being chosen back. That is not a small thing.

If you want to share this book with your partner now — you can. The chapters are still here. And so are you.

What is the most important thing you learned about yourself over these ten weeks?

What has changed — in how you show up, what you understand, or what you're willing to try — since you opened this book?

What is the one skill from this workbook you most want to continue practicing — and what would it look like to make that a daily habit rather than an occasional effort?

What do you most want your partner to know that you haven't yet said clearly?

Is there a moment this week — before the workbook goes on the shelf — when you could say it?

The one habit from this workbook I will maintain regardless of whether my partner is working alongside me:

The early warning signs I will watch for — signals that I have started to drift back into old patterns:

What I will do when I notice those signs (be specific — not 'try harder' but the actual action):

The commitment I'm making to this relationship, stated in my own words, today:

☑ **The Completion Ritual**
☐ Read your Relationship Vision Statement aloud together — or silently, alone if you're on the Solo Track
☐ Each partner: share one moment from the past ten weeks you want to hold onto
☐ Each partner: say one thing to the other that you've been wanting to say and haven't yet
☐ Sign your Relationship Maintenance Plan — make it real with both names on it
☐ Celebration: do something tonight that makes you feel like you — as a couple, or as the person you are becoming in this relationship

The Thing I've Been Wanting to Say
Write it here first, if that helps you say it out loud:

You began this workbook somewhere difficult.

You are not in the same place now.

The relationship you have been building over these ten weeks is not finished. It will never be finished — that's not what relationships are. But it is real, and it is more than it was, and it is yours.

Keep choosing it.

The Couple You Keep Becoming

The relationship you want is not a destination you arrive at. It is a direction you keep choosing.

You began this book somewhere. Maybe alone, on your side of the bed, quietly hoping things could be different. Maybe with your partner, tentative and slightly skeptical, agreeing to try something you weren't sure would work. Maybe as a last-before-last resort. Maybe as a gift from someone who saw something worth saving that you'd temporarily lost sight of.

However you began it, you are ending it as someone who has shown up — for ten weeks, for thirty minutes at a time, for the work that most people know they should do and never quite get to.

That matters. That is not nothing.

What This Work Has Actually Been About
It's tempting to describe a relationship workbook as being about communication skills, or conflict tools, or intimacy exercises. And it is about all of those things. The Soft Startup, the Attunement Ladder, the What's True? exercise, the Love Map Update, the six-second kiss — these are real tools, grounded in real research, and they work when you use them.

But underneath the techniques, what this book has really been asking of you is something simpler and harder. To keep showing up for a relationship even when it's uncomfortable. To keep being honest when dishonesty would be easier. To keep choosing your partner — and yourself — in the small, ordinary, unheroic moments that nobody celebrates and that constitute the actual texture of a shared life.

The couples who thrive are not the ones without problems. They are the ones who have decided — together or one at a time, in the early weeks of a workbook or in the quiet years that follow it — that the relationship is worth the trouble of being honest about it.

That is what you did here. Ten weeks of small decisions. Ten weeks of choosing honesty over comfort, and connection over convenience, and the difficult conversation over the silence that would have been easier.
That is the work. That will always be the work. It doesn't end when the workbook goes on the shelf.

Jordan started doing the weekly check-in without being asked. Not formally — not with a timer and a structured agenda. He just started asking, on Sunday evenings, how Maya was really doing. Not "how was your week" but: "How are you?"

Maya noticed. She mentioned it one Tuesday, almost in passing: "I've been thinking about us more lately. In a good way."

Jordan looked up from his phone. "Me too," he said.

They didn't have a profound conversation that night. They had leftover pasta — Thursday's, reheated — and Maya laughed at something Jordan said. Really laughed, from somewhere genuine, for the first time in longer than she could easily name. Jordan felt it land somewhere in his chest: the particular, irreplaceable weight of being the reason the person you love is laughing.

Neither of them said anything about it. But both of them noticed.
The franchise idea was on the table now — not decided, but no longer secret. Jordan had finally said it out loud, in full, and Maya had listened the way Chapter 4 had asked her to, and then she'd said: "Tell me more about what appeals to you." They had talked for two hours. They had gone to bed not having resolved anything, but feeling — for the first time in years — like they were facing the same direction.

That's what this work leads to: not a perfect relationship, but the kind where you notice each other again. Where you're present enough to feel the moments that used to slip by unregistered. Where the person across the table is still, somehow, someone you're discovering.

A Note on the Path That Brought You Here

For the partner who worked through this book alone:

You have done something quietly extraordinary. You chose to show up for a relationship even when you were uncertain it would be reciprocated. You did the harder work — the one that required you to examine yourself without the validation of a partner doing the same thing beside you — and you kept doing it, week after week, with no guarantee of how things would turn out.

The changes you've made are real. Your partner may not have named them. That doesn't mean they haven't felt them. Individual change in a relationship system always creates ripple effects — in the dynamic, in the atmosphere, in the felt sense each partner has of whether the relationship is moving or standing still. You have been moving it.

Whatever comes next, you know something now that you didn't know ten weeks ago. You know you are capable of this kind of sustained, honest, self-directed work. That knowledge belongs to you — and it will serve you in whatever version of your relationship comes next.

Whatever comes next, you know something now that you didn't know ten weeks ago. You know you are capable of this kind of sustained, honest, self-directed work. That knowledge belongs to you — and it will serve you in whatever version of your relationship comes next.

For the couple who worked through it together:
You have built something together over these ten weeks that most couples never build at all: a shared language for the difficult things, a set of practices you can return to when the ordinary friction of life gets loud, and — perhaps most importantly — the memory that you did this. That when things were hard, you chose to do the work rather than wait for the other person to fix it. That is not a small foundation.

Your Continuation Checklist

The following checklist is not a curriculum. It's a compass. When life gets busy and the structure of the workbook fades, these are the things most worth holding onto — the practices that, done consistently, make the largest difference to the daily texture of a long relationship.
Return to this page when things get hard. You don't have to start over. You just have to find the thing on this list that's been missing, and begin again there.

☑ **Maintaining the Relationship You've Built**

☐ Do the Weekly Check-In ritual at least twice a month — more when things feel tense or distant

☐ Practice at least one genuine Repair Attempt every week — the small ones count as much as the large ones

☐ Keep adding to the Love Map: ask your partner one real question this week that you don't already know the answer to

☐ Return to your Relationship Vision Statement quarterly — it will need updating as you grow

☐ Use the Soft Startup the next time you need to raise something hard — name the feeling, describe the situation, state what you need

☐ Remember the Time-Out Protocol before the next escalation begins, not during it

☐ Revisit this book when things drift — returning is maintenance, not failure

☐ Consider working with a couples therapist if this book has opened doors you want to go deeper through

You are not the same couple who opened this book.

You are not finished becoming.

A great relationship is not something you arrive at. It is something you keep arriving at, every day, in the thousand small moments of choosing — choosing to listen, choosing to speak, choosing to reach across the space that opens between any two people living a full and complicated life.

You know how to do this now.

Keep choosing.

For the Partner Who Arrives Mid-Book

If your partner has been working through this book and you're just joining —
welcome. You don't need to start over, and you don't need to apologize for arriving
late.

Your partner has been doing real work. They have spent weeks examining their own
patterns, practicing new ways of speaking and listening, and trying to show up
differently in ways they may not have been able to name clearly while they were
doing them. The fact that you're here now, reading this page, is itself a form of
showing up. Notice that.

What you need to know to get started:

Each chapter stands largely on its own. You can begin wherever your partner
currently is — Chapter 6, Chapter 8, wherever — and the Together Track exercises in
that chapter will be accessible without having read everything that came before.

That said, three exercises from earlier chapters are worth doing independently, even
if you join late. They take about thirty minutes total and will orient you to the
foundation everything else builds on:

The Relationship Landscape Map — Chapter 1
Ten minutes. Scores the five core dimensions of relationship health. Gives both
partners an instant shared vocabulary for what's working and what needs attention.
The What's True? Exercise — Chapter 2
The three-column exercise separating fact from story. Five to ten minutes on one
recent incident. Shifts the way you engage with the next difficult conversation.
The Attunement Ladder — Chapter 4
The five-rung listening framework. Read it once and try Rungs 1–3 in the next
conversation that matters. The impact is immediate.

When to Seek Professional Support

This workbook is a powerful self-help resource, grounded in research and designed to produce real change when used consistently. It is not a substitute for professional therapy in every situation.

We encourage you to seek a licensed couples therapist if any of the following apply:

Situations where professional support is strongly recommended:

• The relationship involves any form of physical, emotional, or sexual abuse — including coercive control

• Either partner is dealing with active addiction, severe mental illness, or trauma that significantly impairs daily functioning

• There has been recent infidelity that has not been fully disclosed or processed

• After completing this book, you feel stuck and the core patterns haven't shifted

• You are seriously considering separation and want to make the best possible decision with full clarity

• The conversations this book has opened feel too large or too raw to navigate without a professional container

Seeking professional support is not a sign that this workbook failed. It is a sign that you have a clear enough picture of where you are to know what kind of help you need. That clarity is itself progress.

Finding a couples therapist:
The following directories connect you with therapists trained in the evidence-based approaches this workbook draws from:

Gottman Method Therapists
gottman.com/couples/find-a-therapist
Emotionally Focused Therapy (EFT) — ICEEFT Directory
iceeft.com/find-a-therapist
Psychology Today Therapist Finder
psychologytoday.com/us/therapists — filter by 'couples' and your location

Recommended Reading

The following books have directly informed this workbook's approach or offer valuable deeper reading on the subjects it covers. Each is recommended for different reasons — some are research-dense, some are practical, some are both.

Foundation — the research this workbook draws from most directly:

The Seven Principles for Making Marriage Work — John & Julie Gottman The accessible summary of four decades of relationship research. Readable, practical, and the closest thing to a canonical text on what makes long partnerships work. Start here if you want to go deeper on any concept from Chapters 1, 3, 4, or 6.

Hold Me Tight — Sue Johnson The defining popular text on Emotionally Focused Therapy. Johnson's framework of adult attachment and emotional responsiveness underpins much of Chapters 4 and 7. Essential reading for couples where emotional safety and felt connection are the central concern.

On desire, sexuality, and physical intimacy:

Come As You Are — Emily Nagoski The most evidence-based and compassionate book available on female sexuality and desire. Directly relevant to Chapter 7 and the desire discrepancy conversation. Accessible and non-prescriptive.

On attachment and how our histories shape our partnerships:

Attached — Amir Levine & Rachel Heller A readable introduction to adult attachment theory and its practical implications for relationship dynamics. Useful context for Chapter 2's attribution work and Chapter 8's origin story exercises.

Wired for Love — Stan Tatkin Tatkin's neuroscience-informed approach to why partners trigger each other and how to build a secure relationship. Excellent companion to the conflict chapters.

On communication, repair, and rebuilding:

Getting the Love You Want — Harville Hendrix The original couples workbook — still useful, particularly for its structured dialogue exercises and its insight into why we choose the partners we choose.

Love More, Fight Less — Gina Senarighi A warm, practical guide to relationship communication with a focus on reducing reactivity. Good companion reading alongside Chapters 3 through 5.

www.ingramcontent.com/pod-product-compliance
Lightning Source LLC
Chambersburg PA
CBHW080342030726
47595CB00013B/4104